BRAIN WAVES

RELIGIOUS EDUCATION

Celebration

June and Peter Curtis

CONTENTS

Introduction	3 - 4
Value	
Teacher's notes	5 - 6
My Treasures	7
Who is important to me?	8
Rules! Rules! Rules!	9
I belong to ...	10
Good and bad	11
Goodies and baddies	12
Light at Christmas	13
Thanksgiving	
Teacher's notes	14 - 15
Thank you	16
I can	17
What a wonderful world!	18
Creation	19
My world	20
Thanksgiving	21
Remembrance	
Teacher's notes	22 - 23
That reminds me!	24
Happy and sad	25
Food	26
Special to me	27
Help me remember	28
Remember that story?	29
Pesach	30
The passage of time	
Teacher's notes	31 - 32
Happy New Year	33
Looking back	34
New Year Celebrations	35
A Year of feelings	36
When I was born	37
Happy Birthday	38
Joy	
Teacher's notes	39 - 40
Happiness	41
The best day of my life	42
Let's have a party!	43
The best present ever	44
Gifts	45
Special places	46
Festivals	47
Sorrow	
Teacher's notes	48 - 49
What makes me sad?	50
It makes me cry	51
I hurt someone	52
Here is the news	53
Lasting memory	54
A time to reflect	55
Additional resources	56

Folens books are protected by international copyright laws. All rights are reserved. The copyright of all materials in this book, except where otherwise stated, remains the property of the publisher and author(s). No part of this publication may be reproduced, stored in a retrieval system, or transmitted, in any form or by any means, for whatever purpose, without the written permission of Folens Limited.

Folens copymasters do allow photocopying of selected pages of this publication for educational use, providing that this use is within the confines of the purchasing institution. You may make as many copies as you require for classroom use of the pages so marked.

This resource may be used in a variety of ways; however it is not intended that teachers or students should write directly into the book itself.

© 1991 Folens Limited, on behalf of the authors.

Illustrations by Dandi Palmer

First published 1991 by Folens Limited, Dunstable and Dublin.

ISBN 185276073-7

Folens Limited. Apex Business Centre, Boscombe Road, Dunstable, LU5 4RL, England.

Printed by Ashford Colour Press.

THE NATURE OF PRIMARY RELIGIOUS EDUCATION

The 'raw material' of religious enquiry is the questions that human experience raises. We try to make sense of our experiences of ourselves as growing, developing, changing human beings, of our relationships with others and of the world about us in all its infinite variety. Out of this search for meaning are born the ideologies, philosophies and religious systems of the world.

It follows, therefore, that the 'raw material' of Religious Education is not just the developed religious systems of the world (important though they are to R.E.) but the basic human experiences and questions which those religions seek to address. Certainly R.E. wants children to know what answers Muslims, Jews, Christians etc. give to what are sometimes called 'ultimate questions' but it is concerned, too, that they should wrestle for themselves, as far as they are able at any particular stage of their development, with the great human questions such as those of purpose, meaning, value and destiny.

As far as primary school children are concerned, this 'wrestling' will consist largely of reflection on the experiences that give rise to the 'ultimate questions'. From a very early age, children are aware that they are growing and changing, that they are no longer as they were, that they are acquiring new skills, that they are experiencing new emotions, that they are in some respects like other people but in other respects unique. They are beginning to address the question of identity - who (or what) am I? Early on they encounter life and death. It may come through the cycle of nature, pets within the home or school, or through the birth of a new baby in the family or the death of a grandparent. They are beginning to address the questions of origin and destiny - where did I come from and where am I going? In similar ways their experiences require them to begin (perhaps subconsciously at first) to address the questions of meaning and purpose in life, of values and of suffering.

It follows that the starting-point for primary R.E. is the children themselves, their experiences and their attempts to make sense of them. Primary R.E. will seek to help children to understand the world of religion that goes on around them. It will also encourage them to reflect in as great a depth as they are able on the experiences that life brings their way. 'Reflection in depth on experience' (of religion and of life itself) is, perhaps, the best definition we can offer of primary R.E.

CELEBRATION

Against this understanding of the nature of primary R.E. we consider the particular theme of 'celebration'. Religion is full of 'celebration'. Sikhs celebrate the birthday of the founder of their faith, Guru Nanak. Jews celebrate the Passover. Christians celebrate the Eucharist (the Mass or Holy Communion). Hindus celebrate Divali, Buddhists Wesak, Muslims Eid, and so on. So 'celebration' takes us straight to 'celebrations' and to religious 'festivals' of which there are a great many. And, as every primary school teacher knows, festivals provide a natural and successful way into the study of 'explicit' R.E. (the study of what is clearly identifiable as religious belief and practice). Many a classroom and assembly hall will mark the progress of the year by exploring the religious festivals as they come and go.

But this is not another book about festivals. It has not set its objectives in terms of 'covering' the major festivals of which children living in a multi-faith society should be aware. Teachers are not short of such materials (see resources) and are encouraged to use them. But this book is about something more basic. Note the singular of the title. This is a book which first and foremost is about celebration, not celebrations. Its first aim is to help children explore what celebration involves - what the 'ingredients' or 'constituent elements' of celebration are - through reflection on their own experiences as much as on 'religious' events. A consequence of that will be that children should be able to understand religious celebrations better. But that, it must be stressed, is a consequence, not the fundamental objective.

In this publication we have identified six 'ingredients' of celebration. The first, we submit, is essential to all forms of celebration. The others may not be 'essentials' but certainly they occur in celebration with great frequency.

We celebrate something when we affirm its importance. We may choose to do this on a particular day each year, but that is not obligatory. We may show our celebration with parties, new clothes, presents, songs, dances, and special foods, but none of these is essential. What is essential is that the thing celebrated matters. So people can celebrate vastly different events - from the winning of a game to the winning of a war, from the birth of a baby to the anniversary of a grandparent's death, from passing an exam to getting engaged, from Yom Kippur to Purim, from Good Friday to Easter Day.

If to celebrate is to affirm importance (of something or somebody) we have immediately identified our first and essential 'ingredient' - value. At the heart of celebration lies the attaching of value. Unless children understand what it is to attach value to something they will never understand celebration. And when we value something we usually feel gratitude for it, hence our second 'ingredient' - thanksgiving.

Since celebration so frequently involves remembering events or people and since many celebrations are regular (often annual) occurrences or mark key moments in an individual's life, 'remembrance' and 'the passage of time' are our third and fourth ingredients. 'Joy' is the fifth since celebration is so often almost synonymous with rejoicing and happiness. It is important to remember, however, that there can also be a sombre side to celebration as in the celebration of a martyrdom or death. So sorrow is our sixth ingredient and our ingredients may be summed up thus:

It follows from what has been said that there is a very personal element to celebration. Just as worship involves the affirmation of the worth or worthiness of something or somebody, so celebration involves an affirmation of value. It is important (both morally and educationally) not to try to involve children in the affirmation of values to which they do not subscribe. There is a form of celebration, therefore, that is possible and appropriate only for Christians at Christmas and Easter, only for Jews at Passover, only for Sikhs at Baisakhi etc. A Jewish child cannot, and should not be asked to, celebrate Easter in the way a Christian child can. It is possible, however, to celebrate a festival of a religious tradition other than one's own in the sense of recognising (and affirming) the value of that event to (some) other people. There is nothing unacceptable in this - it is sound both educationally and morally - but it is important for the school to ensure that it is asking nothing inappropriate of its children (or staff) and that the integrity of each child, of each adult, and of each religion is being maintained. If that is safeguarded the educational process is sound.

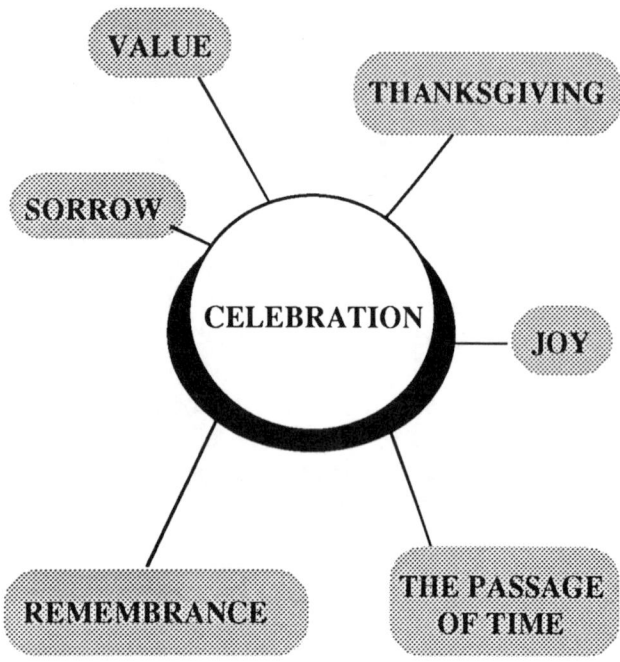

What follows is a series of worksheets relating to each of these six points of focus. In each section, some sheets have Key Stage 1 in mind, others Key Stage 2. The sheets in each section, therefore, are not designed as a series to be used with one group of pupils. They are sequential, rather, in that they point to ways in which, over the time represented by Key Stages 1 and 2, children may be brought into a fuller understanding of that aspect of celebration and of religious celebrations in particular. There are teacher's notes to each sheet, and these contain not only resources on the festivals to which the sheets refer but also some suggestions as to stories from children's fiction which may serve as a way into the sheet's theme.

© 1991 Folens Ltd.

VALUE

The natural egocentricity of young children means that, for most, value begins, at least implicitly, with self. Such children can be encouraged to think about what they themselves value in terms of both people and material possessions. An extension of such thought is to reflect on the influences on their developing sense of value, including, of course, that of parents and of the groups to which the children belong. Older primary children are able to begin to think more broadly and, to some extent, more abstractly, about the wider world and the broad concepts of 'good' and 'bad' in a more ultimate sense and the way religious traditions express such ideas through the myths and stories that so often lie at the heart of religious celebrations. The sheets in this section offer examples of the ways in which such issues may be approached.

Page 7 - My treasures

Encourage the children to talk freely about their personal 'treasures'. If they are able (and willing) let them bring them into school for 'show and tell' sessions. Focus not only on what is important but also why. Who (or what) do they remind you of? Where did they come from? Where do you keep them? Why are they special? Are there recent additions? Have any recently been discarded? Ask the children to think ahead. Will you treasure these for ever? Can you think of things you may want to add later (eg swimming badges, trophies, wedding ring)? Older children might be encouraged to think of non-material 'treasures' (eg memories, friendships).

A way in through story:

Brett M., *Jiggy's Treasure Hunt*, The Medici Society
Hughes S., *Dogger*, Bodley Head/Collins Picture Lion
Keeping C., *Joseph's Yard*, O.U.P.
Ungerer T., *The Three Robbers*, Methuen

Page 8 - Who is important to me?

Discuss who the children consider to be important to them. This is likely to focus initially on family, friends and pets, but could later include a wider range of people who may influence the children's lives (eg teachers, brownie leaders, swimming instructors, religious leaders). Encourage the children to consider why these people are important (care, provision, safety, health, instruction, fun, comfort etc.). Children can also begin to consider how they themselves are important to others (eg in their role as carers for pets or friends to other children).

A way in through story:

Keeping C., *Charlie, Charlotte and the Golden Canary*, O.U.P.
Lobel A., *Frog and Toad Books*, Young Puffin
Secombe H., *Katy and the Nurgla*, Puffin

Page 9 - Rules! Rules! Rules!

One of the reasons why people are important to children is the fact that they provide them with the structure of rules within which they are to live their lives. The sheet could be used as a starting point for discussing rules within the home, attention being paid to the reasons behind the rules (ie the values that undergird the rules - health, safety, training, moral values etc.) as well as to the rules themselves and the consequences of breaking them. Older children may be encouraged to consider the origins of their parents' values (and hence the rules they impose). For some this may include explicitly religious values and their ensuing patterns of behaviour (eg the wearing of the 5 Ks, the eating of halal and kosher foods, regular prayer, ethical standards). Children may also reflect on important people who have passed on their values through their lives, teaching and example (eg Dr. Barnardo, Gandhi, Mother Theresa, Martin Luther King, Henry Dunant as well, of course, as the founders of religions) and thus have influenced national and international 'rules'. It may be appropriate to note that not all examples are good (eg Hitler).

A way in through story:

Aiken J., *Tale of a One-Way Street*, (title story) Book Club Associates
Ritter M., *Mum's Strike*, Magi

Other useful resources:

Faith in Action series, R.M.E.P.
Mayled J., *Family Life* (Religious Topics series), Wayland

Page 10 - I belong to ....

Belonging to a group usually brings with it the requirement to conform to the group's values and often involves promises to obey its rules. Some groups may be specifically religious, others secular. Talk with the children about the 'marks' of group belonging and the practical ways in which they affirm the values of the group (eg registration, enrolment and membership, badges, parade services, special foods, uniforms and dress, customs, group activities, rules). Explore with the children what happens if and when they break the group rules. How do they feel? How important are the rules and promises to them? Older children might consider the promises that parents make on behalf of their children when (eg in infant baptism) they join a religious community.

© 1991 Folens Ltd.

A way in through story:

Bennett O., *A Busy Weekend,* Hamish Hamilton

Useful pupil resources:

Mayled J., *Initiation Rites* (Religious Topics series), Wayland

Teacher resources:

Gregory R. (ed.), *Exploring a Theme: Communities,* C.E.M.

Page 11 - Good and bad

From an early age children begin to develop their thinking about 'good' and 'bad', 'right' and 'wrong'. It is important that they should intellectualise about these concepts but they need the opportunity, too, to respond imaginatively to that process of thought. This sheet invites children to express their thoughts in a symbolic way and thus plays a part in introducing children to the ways in which religion so frequently expresses its essential ideas through the symbolism of art and story. It could be used for either individual or group expression.

A way in through story:

Carew J., *Children of the Sun,* Little, Brown and Co.
Cooper S., *The Dark is Rising,* Bodley Head
Jones T., *Fairy Tales (Why Birds Sing in the Morning),* Puffin

Page 12 - Goodies and baddies

This sheet encourages thought about the way in which 'good' and 'bad' are so frequently represented in stories through characters whom the children quickly identify as the 'goodies' and the 'baddies'. Children can think about the stories, cartoons, TV programmes, films etc. they know in which this theme is a recurring feature - eg Star Wars, Turtles, Tom and Jerry, Robin Hood - and the qualities of the good and bad characters and the ways in which each is represented in the story. This promotes reflection on the values implicit in story and paves the way for consideration of many stories central to religious celebration, eg the story of Rama and Sita.

One possible extension is to invite consideration of the question of whether the story characters are wholly good or bad and of the extent to which this reflects the children's experience of themselves and of other 'real' human beings.

A natural way in:

Through discussion of stories, cartoons etc. within the children's recent experience.

For resources on Divali see page 23.

Page 13 - Light at Christmas

In many religious traditions light and darkness serve as symbols of good and bad. Encourage the children to think why this is so. What are the properties of light? What does it help us to do? What does it make possible in the natural world? What would life be like without it? Children might think of the relationship between light and such things as life, safety, colour, warmth and joy. Discuss the way in which the idea of 'light' is used in everyday speech (eg 'shedding light' on something, a 'flash' of inspiration). This sheet invites consideration of the way in which light is used as a symbol of good in the Christian celebration of Christmas - tree, house and street decorations, candles, the star, haloes and angels. A visit to a church would be valuable and children can describe their own experiences (eg of lighting an advent candle). All of this paves the way for an understanding of such Christian ideas as Jesus as 'Light of the World'. Within Christianity, the story of Saint Lucia will also be worthy of study and comparable lessons on light symbolism might be learned from a consideration of festivals from other faiths, eg Chanukah or Divali.

A way in through story:

Barratt S. (ed.), *The Tinder-box assembly book (The Boy Who Trapped the Sun),* A + C Black

Teacher resources:

Broadbent L. (ed.), *Festivals of Light,* C.E.M.
Tompkins S. (ed.), *Celebrating Christmas,* C.E.M.

Pupil resources:

Berg L., *Christmas* (Celebrations series), Ginn
Blackwood A., *Christmas* (Festivals series), Wayland
Ewens A., *Christmas* (The Living Festivals series), R.M.E.P.
Shannon T., *Christmas and Easter* (The Chichester Project), Lutterworth

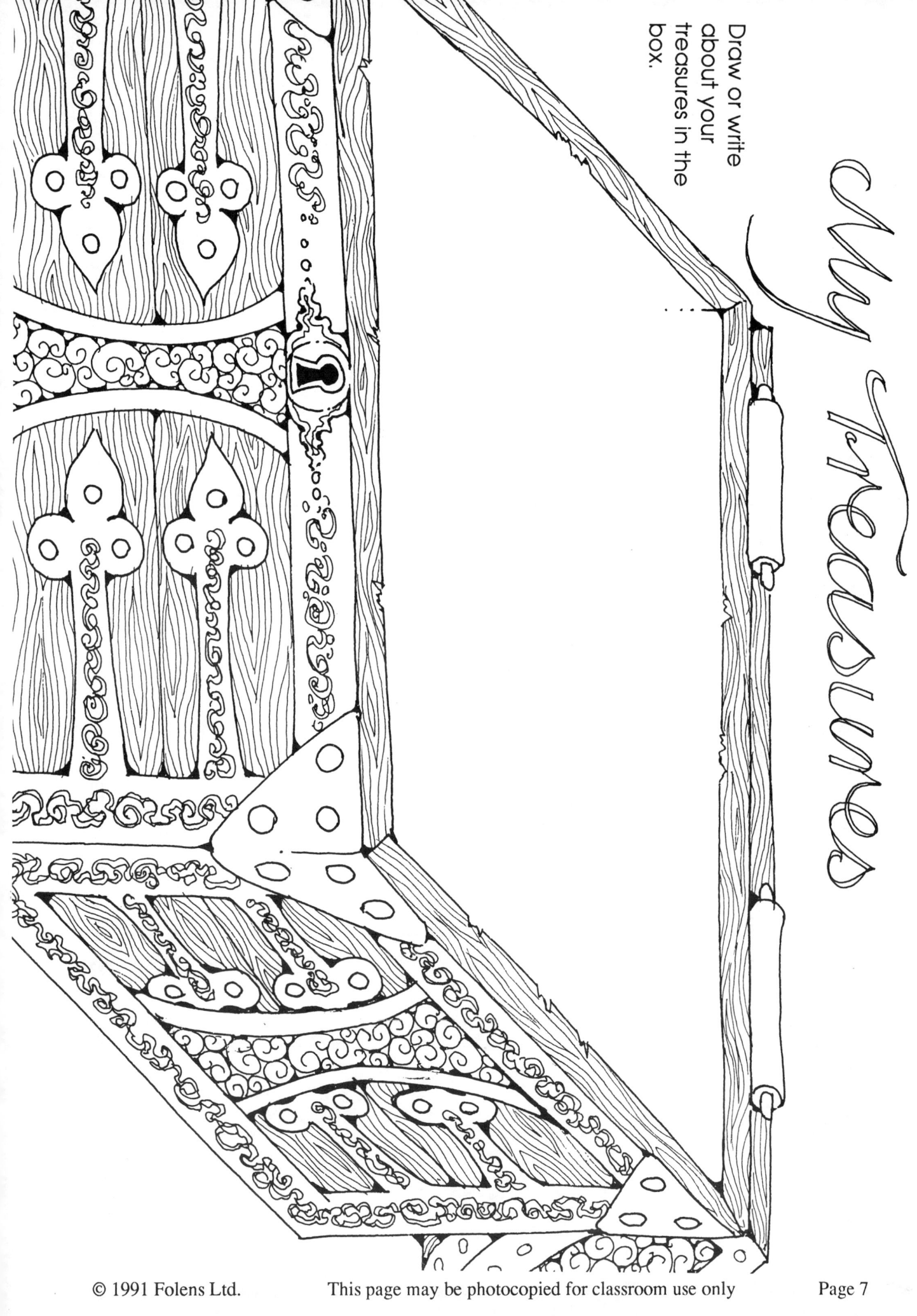

WHO IS IMPORTANT TO ME?

Draw pictures or stick on photographs to show who is important to you.

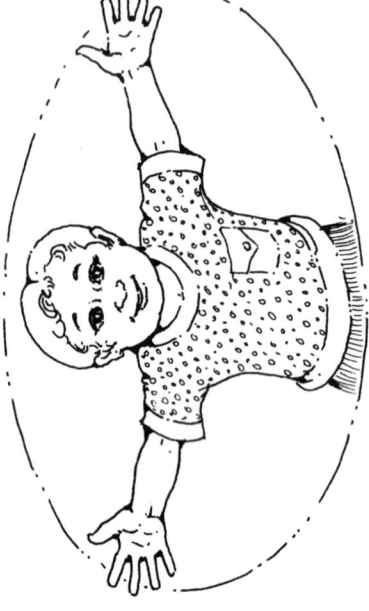

Either tell somebody or write on the other side of this sheet why they are important to you.

Rules! Rules! Rules!

You must

You must not

I belong to . . . . .

Draw a picture or stick on a photograph of what you wear when you go to ...

_____

Do you have to make promises or agree to rules or laws?

Write them out here.

NOW Write or tell about your first day at ...

Make a picture representing good and bad. Use this sheet as a plan for your design.

Will there be a gap in the middle?
Will the two halves touch?
Will the two halves overlap?

NOW

Use your design to create a picture with paints, crayons or collage materials. Explain your picture to friends.

GOODIES and BADDIES

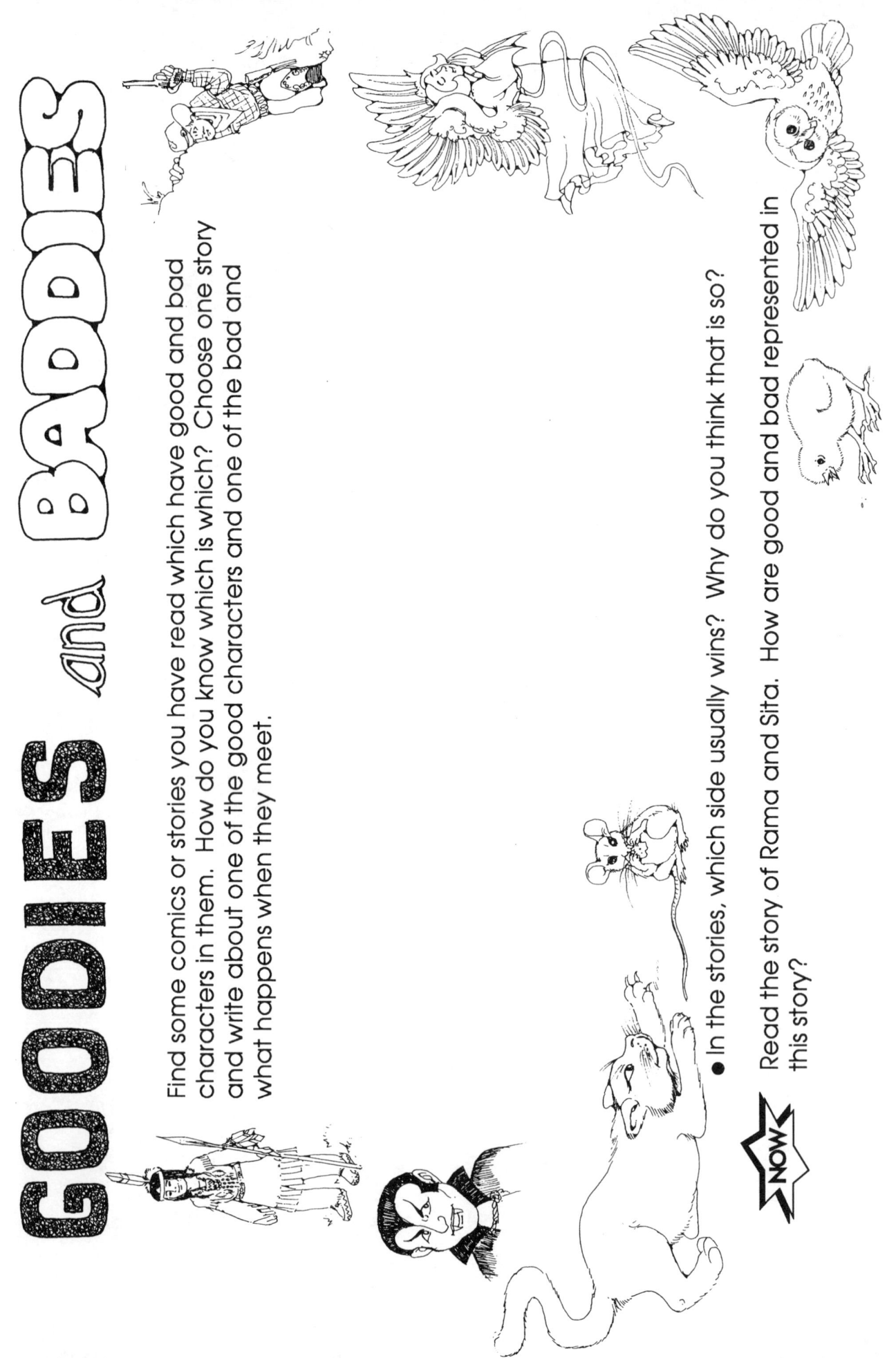

Find some comics or stories you have read which have good and bad characters in them. How do you know which is which? Choose one story and write about one of the good characters and one of the bad and what happens when they meet.

- In the stories, which side usually wins? Why do you think that is so? How are good and bad represented in this story?

Read the story of Rama and Sita. How are good and bad represented in this story?

NOW

Light at Christmas

Some Christians make a Christingle at Christmas because of all it represents. Some of you might like to make one.

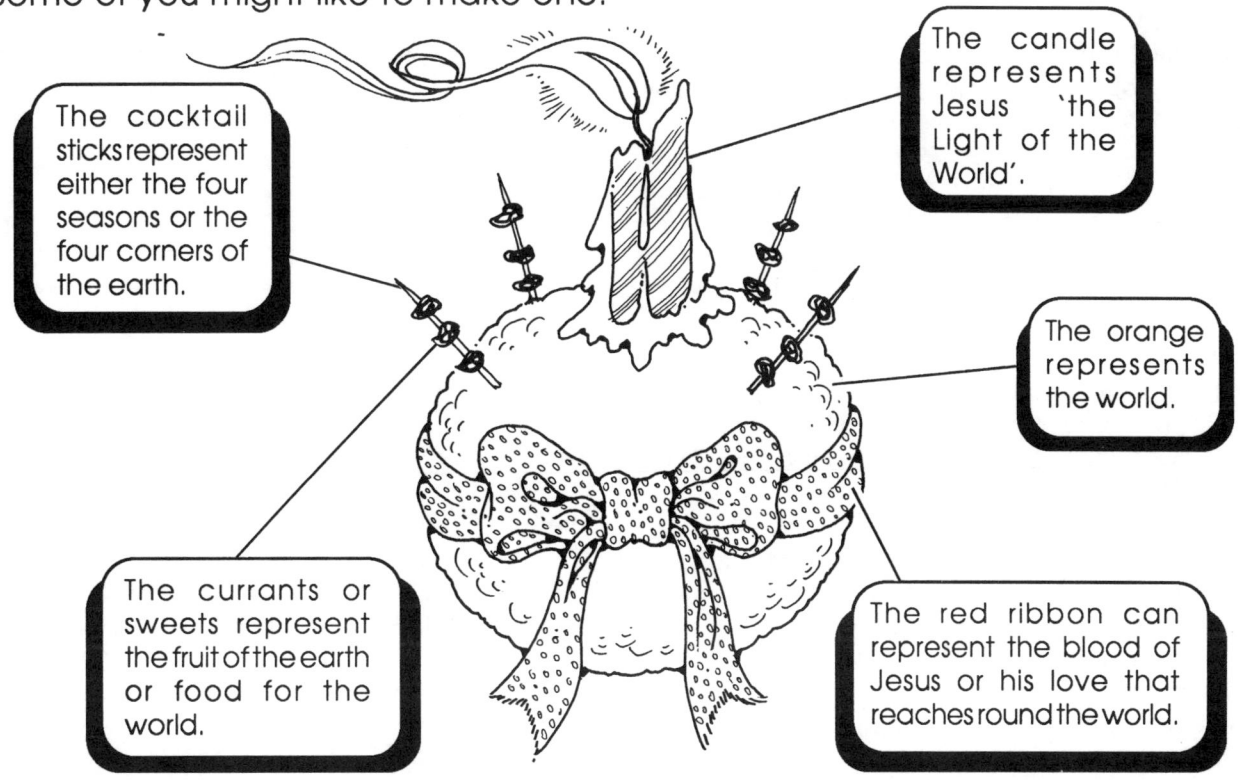

- The candle represents Jesus 'the Light of the World'.
- The cocktail sticks represent either the four seasons or the four corners of the earth.
- The orange represents the world.
- The currants or sweets represent the fruit of the earth or food for the world.
- The red ribbon can represent the blood of Jesus or his love that reaches round the world.

Others could make a collage of Christmas cards that use light in one way or another.

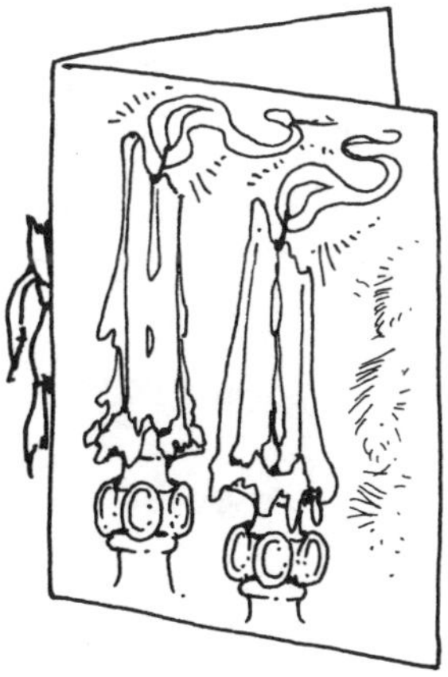

> **NOW**

Can you suggest why Christians refer to Jesus as 'the Light of the World'?

THANKSGIVING

If we value something, we are likely to feel gratitude for it. This gratitude may take the form of wanting to thank the giver (eg as with a birthday present) or it may simply take the form of enjoying and appreciating something when the 'giver' is not so unanimously identifiable (eg the beauty of the natural world). In a specifically religious context, thanksgiving is usually addressed towards one or more deities.

'Thank you' ('ta') is one of the first things children are taught to say. It is then expected in certain contexts. It is easy for saying 'thank you' to become something of a ritual. For it to be genuine (and not just 'good manners') there must be a real valuing of the gift. If children are to understand thanksgiving within the context of religious celebration they must first have genuine experience of being thankful and of being thanked. In young children's experience this is closely linked to praising and being praised for their achievements.

In the explicit world of religion there are many forms of thanksgiving - for the completion of a pilgrimage or fast, for an answer to prayer, for the means of salvation etc. One of the commonest forms of thanksgiving, however, is for creation itself, for the natural world in all its beauty and splendour and for its provision of the necessities of life. Most typically this is seen in the form of 'harvest thanksgivings'. Such 'thanksgiving' involves a response to the natural world and recognition of responsibility for its proper stewardship. These are the themes introduced by the sheets in this section.

Page 16 - Thank you

Encourage the children to recall and talk about the times when they have said 'thank you' or when they have been thanked for something they have said or done. These can be recorded pictorially or in written form on the sheet. They can reflect not only the familiar times of giving and receiving presents (birthdays, Christmas, Eid, Chanukah, Divali) but also the moments of 'spontaneous' thanks including non-material 'gifts' (eg acts of kindness or helpfulness). Ask the children how they felt. Were the thanks really genuine? Older children can be encouraged to reflect on things that might easily be taken for granted (eg home, food, clothes) and on why they feel gratitude or others have felt gratitude towards them.

A way in through story:

Cresswell H., *The Beetle Hunt*, Longman Young Books
Solomon J., *Gifts and Almonds*, Hamish Hamilton
Taylor J. and Ingleby T., *Messy Malcolm's Dream*, World's Work

© 1991 Folens Ltd.

Page 17 - I can ....

Let the children talk about their achievements so far (eg tying shoe laces, swimming, reading, representing the school) and record them on the sheet. Which pleased them most? How did they feel at the moment of achievement? Did they feel that they wanted to thank somebody (eg teacher, parent, instructor, friend)? What were the reactions of their parents, teachers or friends? How did that make them feel? Then let them choose a friend whose achievements they can list. Add them to the sheet. Were they pleased at their friend's achievements or did they have some other feelings?

A way in through story:

Castor H., *Fat Puss and Friends*, Puffin
Duvoisin R., *The Importance of Crocus*, Bodley Head
Gillham B., *And so can I*, Magnet
Hutchins P., *Happy Birthday, Sam*, Bodley Head
McPhail D., *Something Special*, Blackie

Page 18 - What a Wonderful World!

Without ignoring the 'darker' side of nature (eg the natural disaster, the survival of the fittest, the beast of prey), children should be encouraged to appreciate what they find beautiful and wonderful in the natural world. But the response to the world must be the child's not the teacher's! One person's 'marvel' may be another's source of fear (worms, snakes, spiders!). This sheet (completed individually or in groups) invites the children to make their own response to the world around them, to express that response in a variety of art forms and to share it with others. Their creations might have a seasonal theme and be the focus of a display or of an assembly. The children will need time to explore their ideas, to collect natural objects and to reflect on their creations. Not all may wish to share their responses publicly and the right to privacy should be respected. Follow-up discussion may focus on the 'beauty' of non-natural objects.

A way in through story:

Carle E., *The Tiny Seed*, Hodder and Stoughton
Keeping C., *Inter-City*, O.U.P.
Rogers M., *Green is Beautiful*, Anderson Press

Teacher resources:

Lowndes (Evans) J. (ed.), *Exploring a Theme: Gifts and Gift Bringers*, C.E.M.

Page 19 - Creation

One of the questions that fascinates children is that of creation. At first it may be 'How did I begin?' Later it may

Page 14

become 'How did the world begin?' This is also one of the 'ultimate' questions religion asks and children should be aware that creation is an object of religious speculation. Religions often ascribe creation to a deity and thanksgiving for the created world is a natural response. For this sheet teachers will require access to a range of creation stories from a variety of cultures but other stories from children's fiction, eg the account of the creation of Narnia in C.S. Lewis's 'The Magician's Nephew', are equally valuable. In groups, children will find and present information about a number of religions and cultures and consider what can be learned from these stories about the people's understanding of the natural world.

Useful resources for pupils:

Cherry H. and McLeish K., *In the Beginning: Creation Myths from Around the World*, Longman
Creation Stories wallcharts 1 and 2, Pictorial charts, Educational Trust
Maclagan D., *Creation Myths*, Thames and Hudson
Mayled J., *Creation Stories*, Wayland

Teacher resources:

Evans-Lowndes J. (ed.), *Exploring a Theme: The Environment*, C.E.M.

Page 20 - My World

This sheet invites children to turn from others' perceptions of the world to their own vision of how the world ought to be. It thus offers children the opportunity to express their own personal sense of value. Should the world be beautiful or purely functional? Should there be equality or should wealth and poverty exist side by side? While children need to recognise the nature of the world as it is, they should also be stimulated to think about how they would wish the world to be, what they can do to help to achieve those aims and how that 'utopia' might be maintained.

A way in through story:

Baker J., *Where the Forest Meets the Sea*, Julia MacRae Books
Davidson L., *Under Plum Lake*, Puffin
Foreman M., *Dinosaurs and All That Rubbish*, Picture Puffin
Foreman M., *One World*, Anderson Press
Harranth W. and Palecek, *The Wonderful Meadow*, Dennis Dobson
Troughton J., *Tortoise's Dream*, Blackie
Umansky K., *Tiger and Me*, Hutchinson

Page 21 - Thanksgiving

This sheet offers children the opportunity to explore in some detail the way in which the theme of 'thanksgiving' (for a variety of different 'gifts') is taken up in an explicitly religious way. The festivals chosen are harvest, which traditionally focuses on thanksgiving for the 'fruits of the earth' but is now increasingly extended to reflect thanksgiving for the 'products' of industry and technology rather than just of the land, Shavuot, which centres on thanksgiving for the Torah, the Law by which devout Jews regulate their lives because of their belief that it contains all the rules necessary for living in accordance with God's requirements, and Eid-ul-Fitr, which comes at the end of the month-long fast of Ramadan and expresses thanksgiving for the successful completion of the fast. The sheet could be completed individually or in groups with findings shared. Again the end products could be displayed within the classroom or as a focal point for an assembly. (Teachers should remember to avoid representational art on the Eid card. This can be turned into an informative discussion point.)

The full text of the Ten Commandments can be found in Exodus 20: 1-17. Since this is rather lengthy, it may be simpler for children to work with the following abbreviated version:

You must worship no God but me.
You must not make any idols, nor bow down and worship them.
You must not misuse my name.
Remember the Sabbath day and keep it holy.
Show respect to your father and mother.
You must not commit murder.
You must not commit adultery.
You must not steal.
You must not accuse anyone falsely.
You must not long for anybody else's house, wife or possessions.

Pupil resources:

Priestley J. and Smith H., *Harvest and Thanksgiving* (The Living Festivals series), R.M.E.P.
Whitlock R., *Harvest and Thanksgiving* (Festivals series), Wayland
Turner R., *Jewish Festivals* (Festivals series), Wayland
Bennett O., *Ramadan and Eid-ul-Fitr* (Festivals series), Macmillan
Cox L., *Eid for Under Fives*, NES Arnold
Hannaford J., *Ramadan and Id-ul-Fitr* (The Living Festivals series), R.M.E.P.
McLeish K., *Eid-ul-Fitr* (Celebrations series), Ginn
Solomon J., *Gifts and Almonds*, Hamish Hamilton

  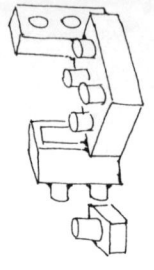 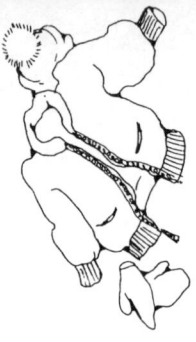 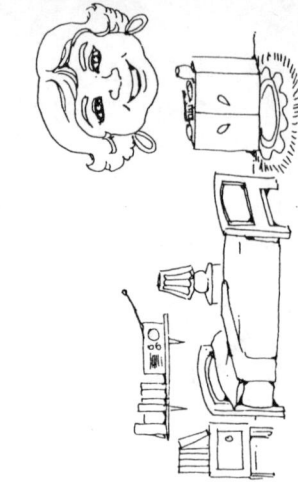

Thank You

I said 'Thank you' to somebody for .....

Somebody said 'Thank you' to me for .....

 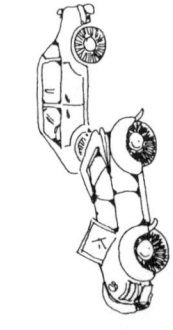  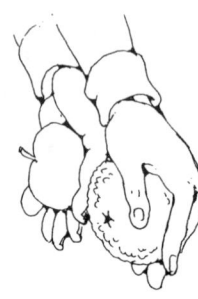  

Draw or write about what you can do.

| Someone said to me _____ |

Choose a friend and draw what your friend can do. They may not be the same things as you.

| I said to my friend _____ |

Find some things which you think are beautiful and create a display with them. The picture above may give you some ideas, but use ideas of your own as well.

Tell your friends about your creation. Draw it or write about it. Make up a song or poem about it.

NOW

Perhaps you can share your creation with the rest of the school. Maybe you can include a creation dance.

Within most religions and cultures you will find ancient stories about creation. See if you can find some of these stories. You may be able to find stories from a number of continents - from India, Africa or from the North American Indians, for example. Take one story and present it to the rest of the class or school. Write here your ideas about how to present it, possibly using dance, drama, mime, music, poetry or songs.

What did the stories tell you about the way the people who told them thought about the world in which they lived?

Would your picture of creation be like this?

Produce your own creation picture in paints or collage or write a creation poem.

Is the world you live in exactly as you would like it to be? Write a story telling your ideas about the creation of a world as you would like it to be. How would you look after that world and make sure it stayed as you wanted it?

Think about
Are things still being created today?

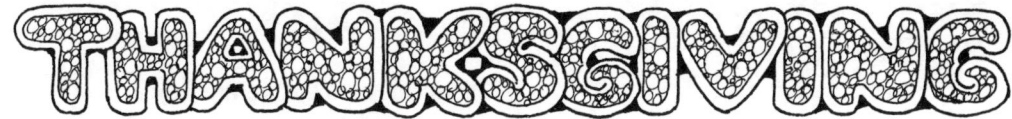
THANKSGIVING

In the Autumn of each year Christians give thanks to God for the harvest.

At Shavuot Jews give thanks for the giving of the law by which they live their lives.

At Eid-ul-Fitr Muslims give thanks for having successfully completed the fast of Ramadan.

See if you can find out what happens at these festivals. Choose one of the suggestions below to make:

1. Make a harvest display of food - real or models

2. Make a scroll with the 10 Commandments written on it.

3. Make an Eid card, or draw round your hand and decorate the shape with crayons or pens, or make some sweets and put them in a decorated box.

© 1991 Folens Ltd.   This page may be photocopied for classroom use only

REMEMBRANCE

Many religious celebrations focus upon the recalling of key incidents from the past. Many Christian celebrations, for example, recall incidents from the life of Jesus. Jewish celebrations often reflect key events in Jewish history, many of them associated with the exodus from Egypt, the wilderness wandering and the reception of the Law. A prerequisite for children's understanding of the significance of such festivals is an appreciation of the importance in their own lives of the remembering of special moments and of the way in which special objects can act as aids to memory.

Page 24 - That reminds me!

Encourage the children to explore the importance of memories by focusing upon their recollections of a past holiday. What memories and feelings does this evoke? In discussion, help the children to distinguish between memories that are preserved solely in their minds and those that are associated with objects that they have brought home (eg shells, pictures, photographs, souvenirs). Let the children appreciate that such objects may be of little value in themselves but nonetheless act as triggers to valued memories. In this way the ground is being prepared for an understanding of the symbolic value of objects in religious celebrations which commemorate past events.

A way in through story:

Flanders J. and Harris C., *My Class Goes to the Seaside*, Franklin Watts
Solomon J., *A Day by the Sea*, Hamish Hamilton

Page 25 - Happy and sad

Memories, of course, are not always happy. There are sad as well as happy events commemorated in religious celebrations. Children need to explore this mixed nature of memories and to recognise that both the happy and the sad have their importance. Which do they remember the better, happy or sad moments from the past? Can they suggest why? By asking parents what happy and sad memories they have from their early childhood children can come to appreciate the role memories can play over a longer period.

A way in through story:

Fox M., *Wilfred Gordon McDonald Partridge*, Viking Kestrel

Page 26 - Food

This sheet helps the children appreciate the way in which particular foods can remind them of special occasions and thus, by implication, the symbolic significance of those foods. This paves the way for an appreciation of the symbolic use of food in such religious celebrations as Pesach and the Eucharist. Children can be encouraged to reflect on the feelings those special foods evoke and whether they are eaten in any special way.

A way in through story:

Pragoff F., *The Birthday Party*, Dent and Sons
Solomon J., *Kate's Party*, Hamish Hamilton

Teacher resources:

Gregory R. (ed.), *Exploring a Theme: Food*, C.E.M.
Paraiso A. and Mayled J., *Soul Cakes and Shish Kebabs*, R.M.E.P.
Ridgway J., *Festive Occasions*, O.U.P.

Page 27 - Special to me

Use this sheet to help children recall key events in their lives so far (eg birthdays, holidays, 'firsts' like starting school or Brownies, or playing for the school team) that are of particular personal importance. Why are those events of such importance? Do they consider them to be worthy of celebration? How would they celebrate them? How did they make them feel? Do they often feel like that? Why are these events special?

A way in through story:

Breinburg P., *My Brother Sean*, Picture Puffin

Page 28 - Help me remember
and
Page 29 - Remember that story?

At the heart of many religious celebrations lie key stories either about the religion's founder or about some important moment in the religion's history. The telling of these stories (often, though not necessarily, in an annual cycle) matters to the believers. And often it is the case that there are objects that are particularly associated with the celebrations and which would act as 'visual aids' in the narration of the story - the nine-branched Chanukiyah or the dreidel at Chanukah, the diva at Divali, the crib and the various figures at Christmas, the etrog and the lulav at Succot etc.

Prior to use of these sheets, a game of Chinese whispers would help children see how stories can change through

© 1991 Folens Ltd.

the process of oral transmission. Or, working in pairs, partners could tell and retell stories to each other. Discuss whether it would help in the retelling of the story if the children had objects that acted as aids to memory. This activity and the accompanying sheets help children to explore the relationship between story and key objects in both secular and religious contexts.

One way into thinking about the Christian Holy Communion with younger children would be to consider how in Susan Varley's 'Badger's Parting Gifts' the animals found that as they met together they treasured not only the parting gifts Badger had given but also all their other memories of their lost friend. Alternatively, there may be somebody who has recently left the school or a pet that has died. Together the children could remember and tell stories about that person or pet. They may have some material 'reminders' that they can show. In some school contexts it may be appropriate for the children to make a meal of bread and fruit-juice wine and to share it together as they tell stories about Jesus.

Pupil resources:

Aunins A. and Bhatti R., *Chinese New Year*, NES Arnold
Bancroft A., *Chinese New Year* (The Living Festivals series), R.M.E.P.
Bennett O., *Chinese New Year* (Festival series), Macmillan
McLeish K., *Chinese New Year* (Celebrations series), Ginn
Smith L., *Dat's New Year* (Celebrations series), A+C Black
Bennett O., *Diwali* (Festival series), Macmillan
Candappa B., *Diwali* (Celebrations series), Ginn
Deshpande C., *Diwali* (Celebrations series), A+C Black
Marsh H., *Divali* (The Living Festivals series), R.M.E.P.
Solomon J., *Sweet-Tooth Sunil*, Hamish Hamilton
Berg L., *Hanukka* (Celebrations series), Ginn
Scholefield L., *Chanukah* (The Living Festivals series), R.M.E.P.
Rankin J., *The Eucharist* (The Chichester Project), Lutterworth

Page 30 - Pesach

This sheet brings together the themes that have run through this section as a whole - the remembrance of key events which are essential to the origins of a religion, in this case the Jewish faith, the regular celebration of which involves the telling of a story. Special symbolic foods are used as aids in the telling of the story. There is also a mixture of emotions. For the Jew at Pesach there is both the bitterness of the collective memory of slavery and the joy of escape, of the saving hand of God seen in history and of the covenant relationship with God. The sheet acts as a way into consideration of this important Jewish celebration.

It is normal to have six symbolic foods on the Seder Plate:

1. A lamb shank bone - a reminder of the lambs that were killed when the Hebrews escaped from Egypt and also of the Egyptians who died. (See Exodus, chapter 12.)
2. A roasted egg - a symbol of life and of destiny.
3. Bitter herbs (often horseradish) - a reminder of the bitter experiences of the Hebrew slaves in Egypt.
4. Salt water - reminiscent of the tears shed by the Jews' ancestors in Egypt.
5. Charoset (a mixture including grated apples, almonds or other nuts, spices and wine) - a 'paste' that represents the 'mortar' used by the Hebrew slaves in Egypt in their building work; its sweet taste also reminds Jews of the good things God did for them.
6. A spring vegetable (usually parsley or lettuce) - this represents hope, new life and God's provision for his people in the wilderness.

Also used in the seder meal are matzos (unleavened bread) and wine. The matzos remind Jews that they left Egypt hastily; they had no time to bake bread with yeast for the yeast had no time to rise.

Pupil resources:

Cashman G.F., *Jewish Days and Holidays*, SBS Publishing
Hannigan L., *Sam's Passover* (Celebrations series), A+C Black
Lawton C., *Matza and Bitter Herbs*, Hamish Hamilton
Marcus A.F. and Zwerin R.A., *But This Night Is Different: A Seder Experience*, Union of American Hebrew Congregations
Scholefield L., *Passover* (The Living Festivals series), R.M.E.P.
Turner R., *Jewish Festivals* (Festivals series), Wayland

That Reminds Me!

Draw or write your memories in the case.

My holiday memories.

Look at each memory. Draw a red ring round it if you brought something home that will help you to remember it. Make a list here of what is left.

Do you think bringing something home will help you remember longer?

Happy and Sad

Memories can be happy or sad.

I remember when ...

Happy times

Sad times

Ask your Mum or Dad what happy memories they have of when they were your age. Do they remember any sad times? Draw or write about one of each.

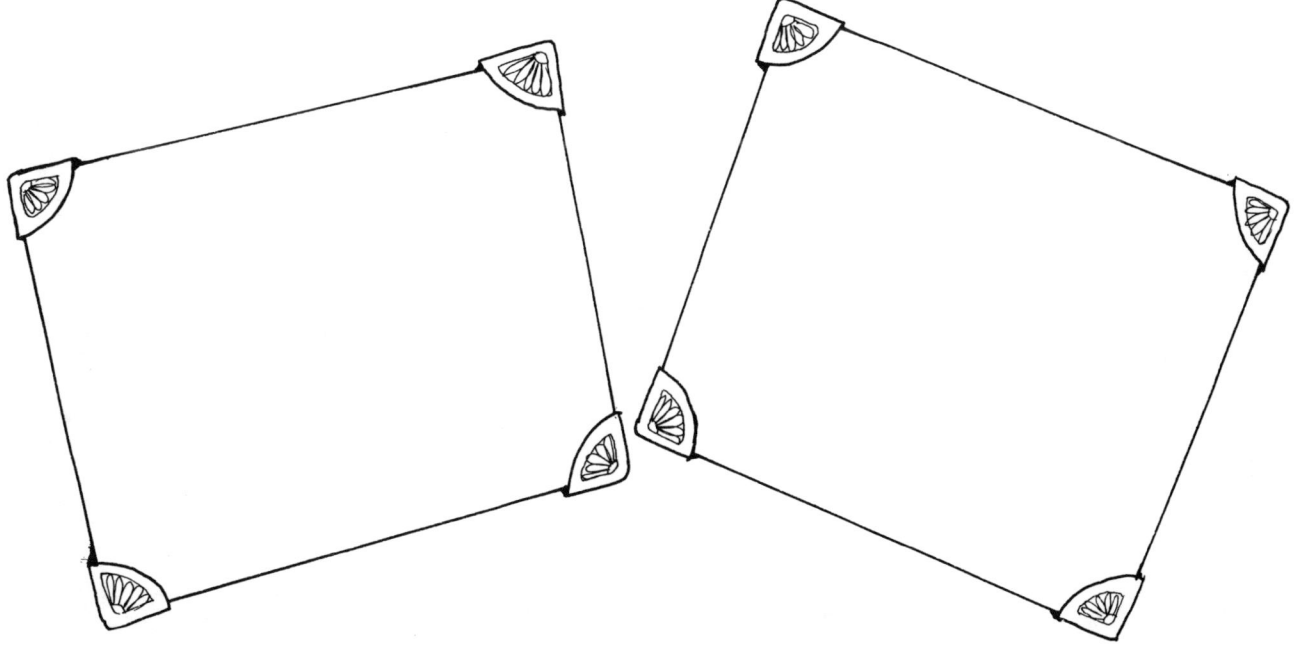

FOOD

_____ reminds me of

_____

_____

_____ reminds me of

_____

_____

NOW Draw other foods which remind you of some special occasion.

Special to Me

Fill the cake with some other special occasions in your life so far.

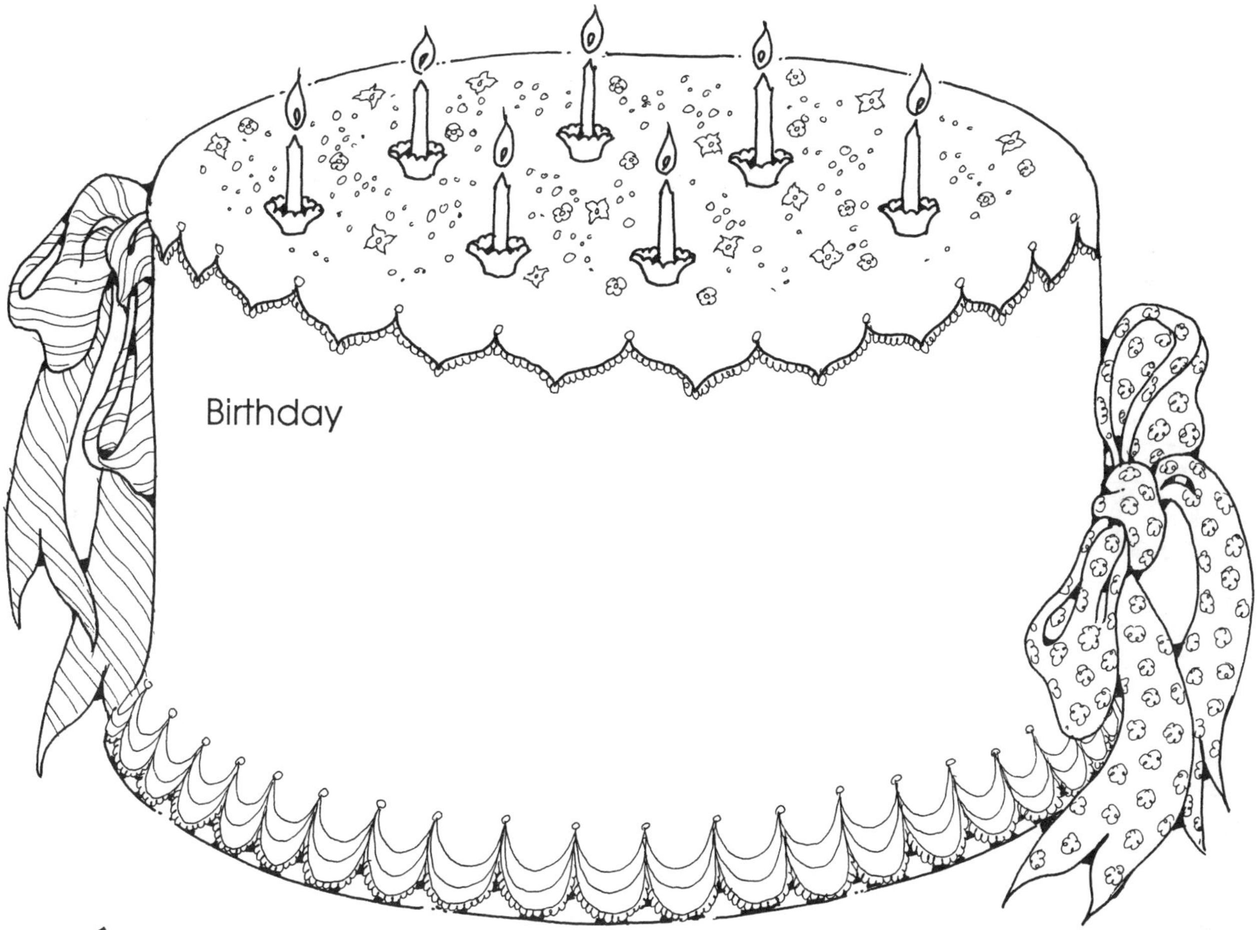

Birthday

 Write about the one you remember most clearly. Can you say why you remember it well? What made it so special?

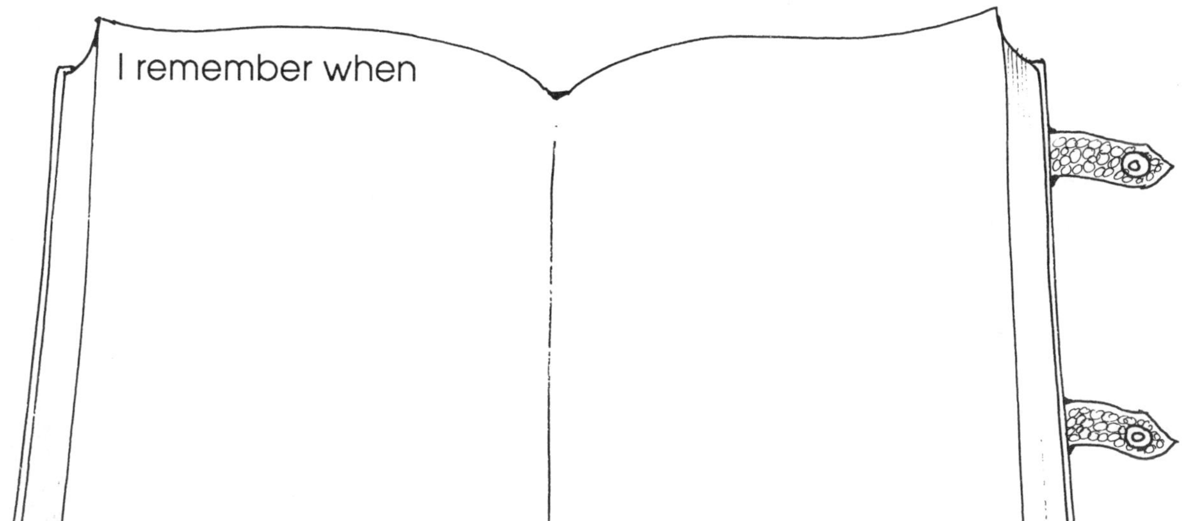

I remember when

© 1991 Folens Ltd.   This page may be photocopied for classroom use only   Page 27

Help Me Remember

Choose a well known story. In the boxes draw objects which are vital to the story and which will help in the retelling of the story.

Give the pictures to a friend. Can they recognize the story from the pictures? Ask them to retell the story.

REMEMBER THAT STORY?

Find the stories that are told at Divali, Chinese New Year and Chanukah. How have they been remembered down the years? Draw the objects that you think would be the most helpful as a reminder of each story.

| Divali | Chinese New Year | Chanukah |

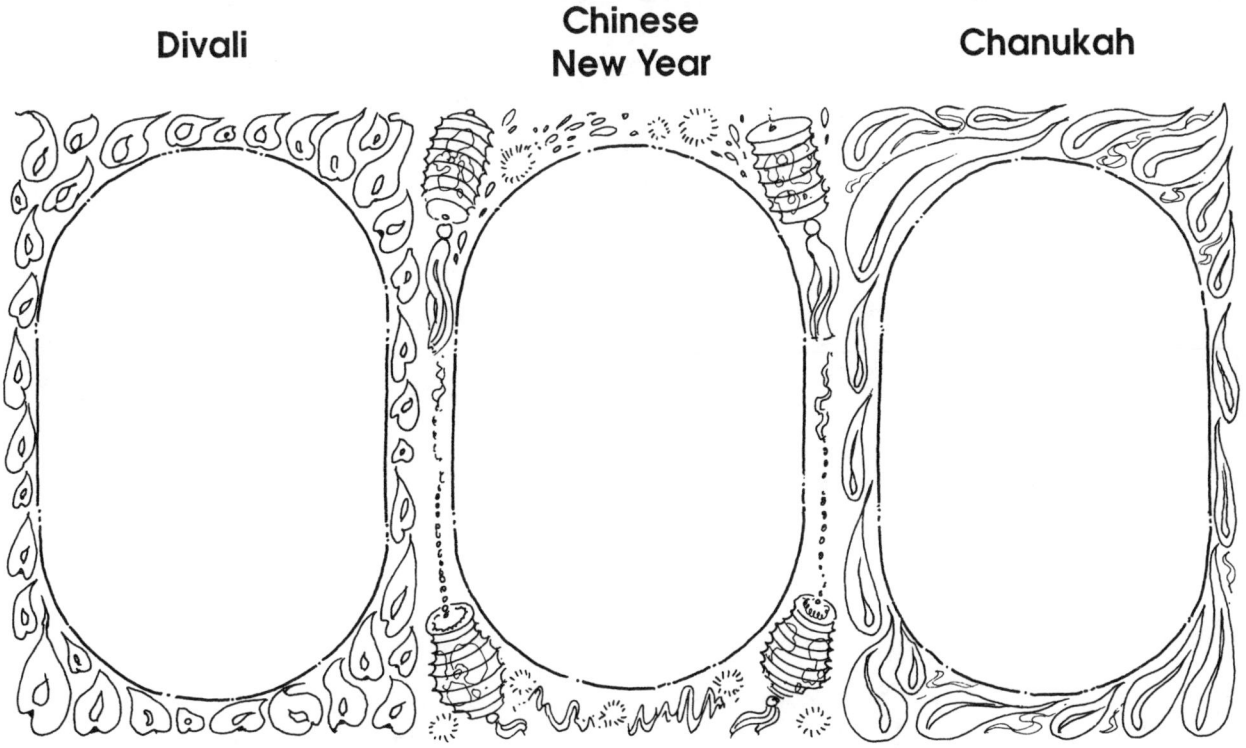

One way in which Christians remember Jesus is by sharing bread and wine in a service called "Holy Communion". The bread and wine remind them of Jesus' last meal with his friends. Christians call this the Last Supper. Jesus asked his friends to do this as a way of remembering him after he had died.

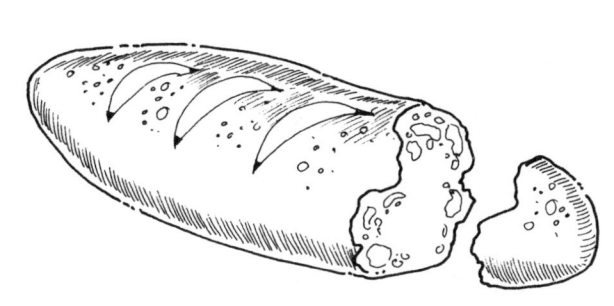 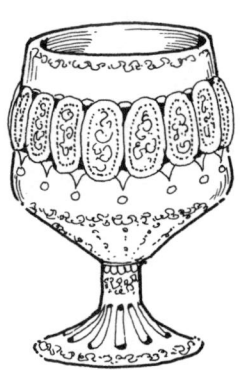

 What other stories about Jesus do you think Christians might think about as they eat the bread and wine? Tell any that you know.

Pesach

"Why is this night different from all other nights?"

This is the question the youngest boy in a Jewish family will ask his father at Pesach. You may know this festival by the name "Passover". One reason this night is different is because of the special food that is used.

At the Passover meal there is a special plate with foods that remind the family of the Passover story.

 Find out and draw what goes on each section of the plate. What part of the story does each represent?

THE PASSAGE OF TIME

In two obvious respects the passage of time is important in religious celebration. First, many festivals (indeed, the majority) occur in an annual cycle so the passing of the year serves as a reminder to the faithful of key aspects of their religion. Second, there are rites and ceremonies (we call them 'rites of passage') which mark the transition from one stage of life to the next, including, of course, entry into and departure from life itself.

Children are capable even at an early age of looking forward with eagerness and anticipation and of looking back and reflecting on the past. Similarly they can appreciate that certain times are associated not just with events but also with feelings. There is an 'emotional' as well as an 'activity' side to the year. Children are capable, too, of recognising that lives have key events and that we mark such events with special ceremonies. All of these are abilities that should be fostered both in their own right and for their potential in helping children to understand religious celebrations.

Page 33 - Happy New Year

The beginning of a new year is always an exciting time. Children can be encouraged to think about the year that lies ahead. There will be things that they know, or hope, will happen to them. They may hope to be a certain height, to learn a new skill (like that already possessed by an older sister, brother or friend), to do something for the first time or to join a new group. So the year that lies ahead will be punctuated with high points for them personally. This mental picture of a year with ' key moments' is mirrored in the religious year by feasts and festivals commemorating and celebrating people, events and beliefs central to the religion concerned. The sense of anticipation and feeling of high emotion as children look forward to new experiences is likewise mirrored in the world of religious celebration.

This sheet may require plenty of accompanying oral work to stimulate children's thinking about the year that lies ahead and all the possibilities it contains. Take care not to impose adult values on the children. Many a parent has felt frustration that the expensive holiday abroad features less in a child's thoughts than joining brownies! To be of value the children's response to this sheet must be genuinely their own.

A way in through story:

McDonnell C., *Lucky Charms and Birthday Wishes*, Puffin
Solomon J., *Berron's Tooth*, Hamish Hamilton

Page 34 - Looking back

To look forward and to anticipate in a sense of excitement and adventure is important. But perhaps it is even more important to look back and to reflect - to take stock and to get things into perspective. In a religious context reflection is a pre-requisite for thanksgiving, for confession and for intercession - three essential elements of the religious life. It is customary to have reflective times of the religious year (Lent, Ramadan, the period from Rosh Hashanah to Yom Kippur) associated with penitence and new resolve - see p.55 and the associated teacher notes (p.49).

The ability to reflect on one's 'performance' in life can begin early. This sheet (which, again, invites the support of considerable oral work both among the children themselves and between children and teacher) offers, particularly if coupled with the last, one way of stimulating reflection by focusing on what has and what has not been achieved in the year now ending. It is important that reflection should pick up both successes and failures, both happy and sad moments. It isn't essential that everything should be recorded in the letter. The important thing is that the thinking should take place and that the letter should reflect something which is of real importance to the child.

A way in through story:

Morris A. and Larson H., *Uzma's Photo Album*, A+C Black

Page 35 - New Year celebrations

This sheet takes children explicitly into the world of religious new year celebrations (which, of course, occur at various times in the calendar year). Children can work individually, but group work may prove more productive in view of the additional discussion engendered. In addition to finding out the 'facts' about the celebrations, children should be encouraged to think about their 'emotional' side. What does the event mean to those who take part? How do they feel? Why does it matter to them? Let the children share their findings. This will permit a focus of attention on common elements in the celebrations as well as on differences. Why, for example, are sweet foods often eaten at such celebrations? Can children see this as a symbol of the wish for health and prosperity and for a 'sweet' year to come?

Pupil resources:

Blackwood A., *New Year* (Festivals series), Wayland
Cole W.O. and Sambhi P.S., *Baisakhi* (The Living Festivals series), R.M.E.P.
Ewens A., *Advent* (The Living Festivals series), R.M.E.P.
Kapoor S.S., *Sikh Festivals* (Festivals series), Wayland
Solomon J., *Sweet-Tooth Sunil*, Hamish Hamilton

© 1991 Folens Ltd.

Solomon J., *Bobbi's New Year*, Hamish Hamilton
Turner R., *Jewish Festivals* (Festivals series), Wayland

Page 36 - A Year of feelings

All primary school teachers will reflect the passage of the year in the course of their teaching. One of the earliest ways in which young children meet the ideas of the 'cycle' of the year is through the four seasons with their differing weather patterns reflected in the appearance of the natural world. All of this is helpful in terms of children's understanding of the annual cycle of religious festivals. But it is important, too, to build up an appreciation of the fact that there is a 'feelings' side to the year. We may feel differently about various periods of and events in the 'natural' year. Do we feel more gloomy in the dark days of winter when the natural world seems dead? But what if our birthday comes in winter? Are we more hopeful in spring when the world is 'waking up', more relaxed in summer sunshine and thankful in the autumn when harvest time comes around? And similarly there are feelings associated with events and periods in the religious year. This sheet is designed to help children explore the 'feelings' side of the passage of time and can provide a stimulus to a great deal of oral work as well as creative activity.

A way in through story:

Dupasquier P., *Our House on the Hill*, Andersen Press
Keeping C., *Joseph's Yard*, O.U.P.
Skargon Y., *Conker Tree*, A+C Black

Page 37 - When I was born

A way into 'rites of passage' (ie celebrations of key transitional moments in the passage through life) can come through children thinking back through their lives to date and inquiring about their own birth. For some, this will lead to discussion within the family about religious rites associated with birth and naming. Some may have observed comparable events when younger sisters or brothers were born. There is often a feeling that 'whatever age I am now is the best age' - a feeling beautifully captured by A.A. Milne's poem 'When I was six'. Nonetheless, it is an important extension of this work to look at the future and to recognize that key events lie ahead. This sheet may result in the arrival in the classroom of photos or other mementos which can be displayed with appropriate labelling. Increasingly home videos will be available, too, which (as well as being the source of a good deal of amusement!) will provide valuable information about the rites and customs associated with birth, naming and early childhood in a variety of cultures.

A way through story:

Anholt C., *When I was a Baby*, Little Mammoth

Baskerville J., *New Baby* (Celebrations series), A+C Black
Blakeley M., *Nahda's Family*, A+C Black

Pupil resources:

Mayled J., *Birth Customs* (Religious Topics series), Wayland

Page 38 - Happy Birthday

The celebration of a birthday is, for most children, an annual 'high moment', and they will also, in all probability, be invited to the birthday parties of friends. This naturally stimulates thought about the importance of birthdays, why we celebrate them and whose birthdays we celebrate. From the conclusion that we tend to celebrate the birthdays of those closest and most important to us it is a small step to the appreciation of why birthdays of founders feature significantly among religious celebrations.

Discussion of what children would most like to do on their birthday will give them (and their teacher) insight into their developing sense of priority and value. Would they like a party? Where would they most like to go? To stay at home or go out? What would they most like to see, do and wear? What would they like to eat? Who would they like to be with on their birthday? To be alone or with friends? What gift would they most like to receive? It can also be used with older children as a way of exploring material and non-material possessions and values. Does being with friends matter more or less than receiving a present? Would good health be a more valuable 'present' than a toy?

A way in through story:

Hutchins P., *Happy Birthday, Sam*, Bodley Head
Keats E.J., *A Letter to Amy*, Bodley Head

Pupil resources:

Ahsan M.M., *Muslim Festivals* (Festivals series), Wayland
Bancroft A., *Festivals of the Buddha* (The Living Festivals series), R.M.E.P.
Davidson M., *Guru Nanak's Birthday* (The Living Festivals series), R.M.E.P.
Mayled J., *Feasting and Fasting* (Religious Topics series), Wayland
Snelling N., *Buddhist Festivals* (Festivals series), Wayland

For resources on Christmas see page 6.

Happy New Year

What are your hopes for the new year?

What things will you learn to do?

I am looking forward to .....

Keep this sheet so you can look back and see what you achieved.

Looking Back

Look back at your hopes for the year. Sit quietly, close your eyes and think about whether you achieved your hopes. Did you learn some new things? Were there disappointments?

Write to a friend to tell them about your year.

Dear _____

New Year Celebrations

Baisakhi   **Chinese New Year**

Divali   **Advent**   **Rosh Hashanah**

Find out in groups about these celebrations. Make some objects for a display to illustrate how these celebrations are kept. Here are some clues:

A YEAR OF FEELINGS

Do you have different feelings at different times of the year? Use this sheet to record your ideas about how the seasons make you feel.

WINTER

AUTUMN

SPRING

SUMMER

Talk to some friends and to your parents or other adults to find out their feelings. Find out why they feel as they do. Add their thoughts to yours.

In groups choose one season and create a collage or display, a story, dance or mime, showing some of the feelings you have written down.

When I Was Born

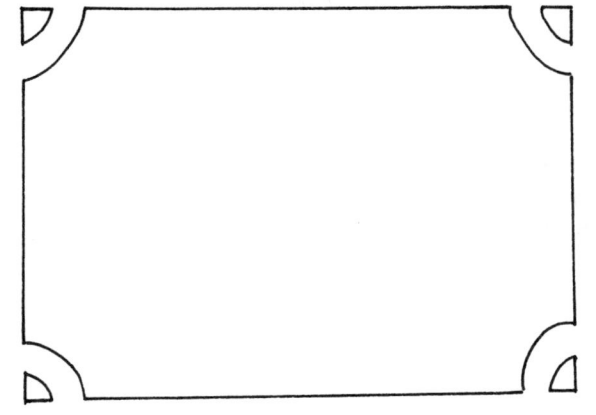

Ask your family what they remember about the day you were born. What stories can they tell you? Have they any photos or other mementos of your first few days you could bring into school to show your friends?

Name _____

Birthday _____

My journey of life so far

NOW — In the last 2 boxes draw 2 things which you hope will happen to you in the future.

© 1991 Folens Ltd.   This page may be photocopied for classroom use only

HAPPY BIRTHDAY

Write down here what you would most like to do on your birthday.

_____
_____
_____
_____
_____

In many religions the followers of the religion celebrate the birthday of the religion's founder or other important people.

> *Christians* celebrate the birth of **Jesus**.
>
> *Sikhs* celebrate the birthday of **Guru Nanak**.
>
> *Muslims* celebrate the birthday of **Muhammad**.
>
> *Buddhists* celebrate the birth of the **Buddha**.
>
> *Hindus* celebrate the birthday of **Lord Ram**.

NOW If you celebrate any of these birthdays write down what you do on that special day. If you don't, see what you can find out about one of them.

JOY

So many celebrations are occasions for joy. They are associated with happiness - it's somebody's birthday, a baby has been born, a new skill has been mastered, a match has been won or a badge earned etc. And this is true not just in the secular world but in the world of religion too. It is perfectly natural to make the celebration of the birth of the founder of a religion a happy and festive occasion. And religious festivals often highlight other sources of rejoicing. Easter and Divali celebrate the victory of good over evil, of light over darkness, of joy over sorrow, of life over death. It is not surprising, therefore, that these occasions are marked by such signs of happiness as special foods (and large meals), new clothes, the giving and receiving of presents, dancing, parties and the like. To understand the joy of religious celebrations children must first experience and reflect on joy in their own lives and, in particular, the joy associated with special occasions.

Page 41 - Happiness

This sheet provides a simple way into thinking about the causes of happiness both for oneself and for other people. Indirectly it invites children to recognise that another person's happiness is as important as their own. To that extent it seeks to break down purely egocentric and selfish thinking. Teachers should help children to appreciate that the 'things' may be material or non-material. Encourage them to think about a range of people to whom they could bring happiness. It is natural for children to begin 'at home', ie with family and friends, but it is desirable to stimulate children's thinking about the wider world including those to whom they can bring happiness without ever meeting them.

One possible extension to this activity is to encourage children to think about the ways in which they can express their happiness. Are words essential? Could they use music, mime or other art forms? How can they show happiness using their bodies - their faces, their arms and hands, their feet, their whole bodies? All such expressions of happiness can be found in religious celebration.

A way in through story:

Gray N., *A Balloon for Grandad*, Orchard Books
Hughes S., *Dogger*, Bodley Head/Collins Picture Lion

Page 42 - The best day of my Life

When asked to recall 'the best day of my life' children will immediately offer a wide range of possibilities, often the first that come to mind. That is fine and each can be thought about. Why were those days good? Because of the enjoyment at the time? Because of their longer term significance? But children can be urged to think more deeply. Eventually they need to identify just one day to write or draw about. This requires careful thought about criteria. What makes one special day more special than others? This sheet offers the opportunity to draw, write and talk about the day of their choice. The crucial thing is that it really is their choice. Adult values should not be allowed to lead the children in a particular direction. Children will only appreciate how Easter, for example, really matters to Christians if they have reflected on what really matters to them.

A way in through story:

Baker J., *Where the Forest Meets the Sea*, Julia MacRae Books
Oram H., *In the Attic*, Andersen Press

Page 43 - Let's have a party!

Having decided what the best day of their lives was, children are now invited to plan a party, to celebrate it and to consider what would be the most appropriate form that party could take. Children should identify somebody whom they would like to invite to the party (eg a relative or a child from another class) and complete the invitation on the sheet which can then be cut out and sent. Then the children can consider an appropriate menu and games which may reflect their chosen days (eg a football cake and some form of football team game or quiz if the 'best day' was 'my first game for the school team'). The thinking in which children are thus having to engage closely mirrors the thinking that lies behind religious celebrations. What is being celebrated? Why is it important? How should it be celebrated? What activities, clothes, food etc. would be most appropriate? Children who have thoughtfully planned a celebration of a significant event in their own lives have the basis of an understanding of the way religious celebrations work.

A way in through story:

Solomon J., *Kate's Party*, Hamish Hamilton.

Page 44 The best present ever

Presents normally give pleasure and 'the best present ever' should be a source of exciting discussion. This sheet, like 'The Best Day of my Life', requires thought about criteria. What makes the best present? Was it the most expensive? The biggest? The one they had looked forward to the longest? The one given by somebody very special? The one that has given pleasure for the longest period?

Some children may think in terms of presents actually

received, others of those they would like to receive. Some may think about presents they have given - and that opens up a whole new set of questions! Again it is important that the children say what they honestly feel, not that they reflect imposed adult values. Thought about presents they would value undergirds an understanding of the place gifts have in both secular and religious celebrations.

A way in through story:

Prater J., *The Gift*, Bodley Head

Page 45 - Gifts

This sheet extends the thinking of the last. Gifts do not have to cost money. Some can be made. Does that decrease their value? Might it even increase it? And do gifts have to be material objects? Are there 'intangibles' that can be given? Recognition that one can 'give' of one's time and abilities is an important extension of the understanding of giving. At the heart of many forms of religious practice is the notion of the 'giving of oneself' (submission, dedication, a 'living sacrifice') to God.

For the purposes of this sheet it might be helpful for children to identify a person who would be the recipient of the gift and an occasion for which the gift would be suitable.

A way in through story:

Cresswell H., *The Beetle Hunt*, Longman Young Books
Keller H., *The Best Present*, Walker Books
Roberts D., *The Gift*, Methuen Children's Books
Solomon J., *A Present for Mum*, Hamish Hamilton

Page 46 - Special places

Religious celebrations are often held in special buildings or other special places (eg routes for processions). The place itself, for the worshipper, is significant because of all its associations. The building (or location) becomes a part of the experience of the celebration. This sense of the 'specialness' of a place is something well within the grasp of even quite young children. All of them will have places that are special to them. It may simply be where they live, where they play, or where they go to school. They may have places that are associated with special memories - 'where my Grandad used to live'. They may be places to which the children go to be alone.

This sheet offers children the opportunity to think, talk and write about or draw places that are special to them and the pleasures those places can bring. It encourages thought about the reasons why places are special. It paves the way for discussion about the specialness of sacred buildings to those who worship and celebrate there and, with older children especially, may lead into discussion of pilgrimage.

A way in through story:

Garland S., *Sam's Cat*, Walker Books
Saltzman M., *No One Knows Where Gobo Goes*, Muppet Press/Sphere Books
Snapes J., *Just the Place for a Cat*, Wheaton
Solomon J., *Shabnam's Day Out*, Hamish Hamilton

Teacher resources:

Gregory R. (ed.), *Exploring a Theme: Places of Worship*, C.E.M.
Gregory R. (ed.), *Exploring a Theme: Journeys*, C.E.M.

Page 47 - Festivals

Like 'New Year Celebrations' (p 35), this sheet is directly concerned with discovery about the living world of religious celebrations. Working individually or in small groups, children can research one of the festivals listed using the sheet to record important points under a number of key headings. Ways of following up this work are manifold. Special foods can be made and shared. Games can be made and played. Stories can be enacted through conventional drama, through dance or through mime. Creative art work can produce a stimulating classroom or assembly display to serve as a backcloth for the sharing of the children's findings with each other or with the rest of the school.

Pupil resources:

Bennett O., *Carnival* (Festival series), Macmillan
Davidson M., *Shrove Tuesday, Ash Wednesday and Mardi Gras* (The Living Festivals series), R.M.E.P.
McLeish K., *Carnival* (Celebration series), Ginn
Menter J., *Carnival*, Hamish Hamilton
Hannaford J., *Holi* (The Living Festival series), R.M.E.P.
Scholefield L., *Succot and Simchat Torah* (The Living Festivals series), R.M.E.P.
Fairbairn N. and Priestley J., *Easter* (The Living Festivals series), R.M.E.P.
Fairbairn N. and Priestley J., *Holy Week* (The Living Festivals series), R.M.E.P.
Fox J., *Easter* (Festivals series), Wayland

For resources on Christmas, Eid-ul-Fitr, Wesak, and The Birthday of Guru Nanak see pages 6, 15 and 32.

© 1991 Folens Ltd.

HAPPINESS

4 things that make me happy

4 ways I can make another person happy

Draw or write about what makes you happy and what you can do to make someone else happy.

© 1991 Folens Ltd. This page may be photocopied for classroom use only Page 41

The Best Day of My Life

Tell your friends how you felt.

Let's have a Party!

Make an invitation to a celebration of the best day of your life.

You are invited to celebrate

_____

on _____

at _____

in _____

Menu

Ideas for party games

THE BEST PRESENT EVER

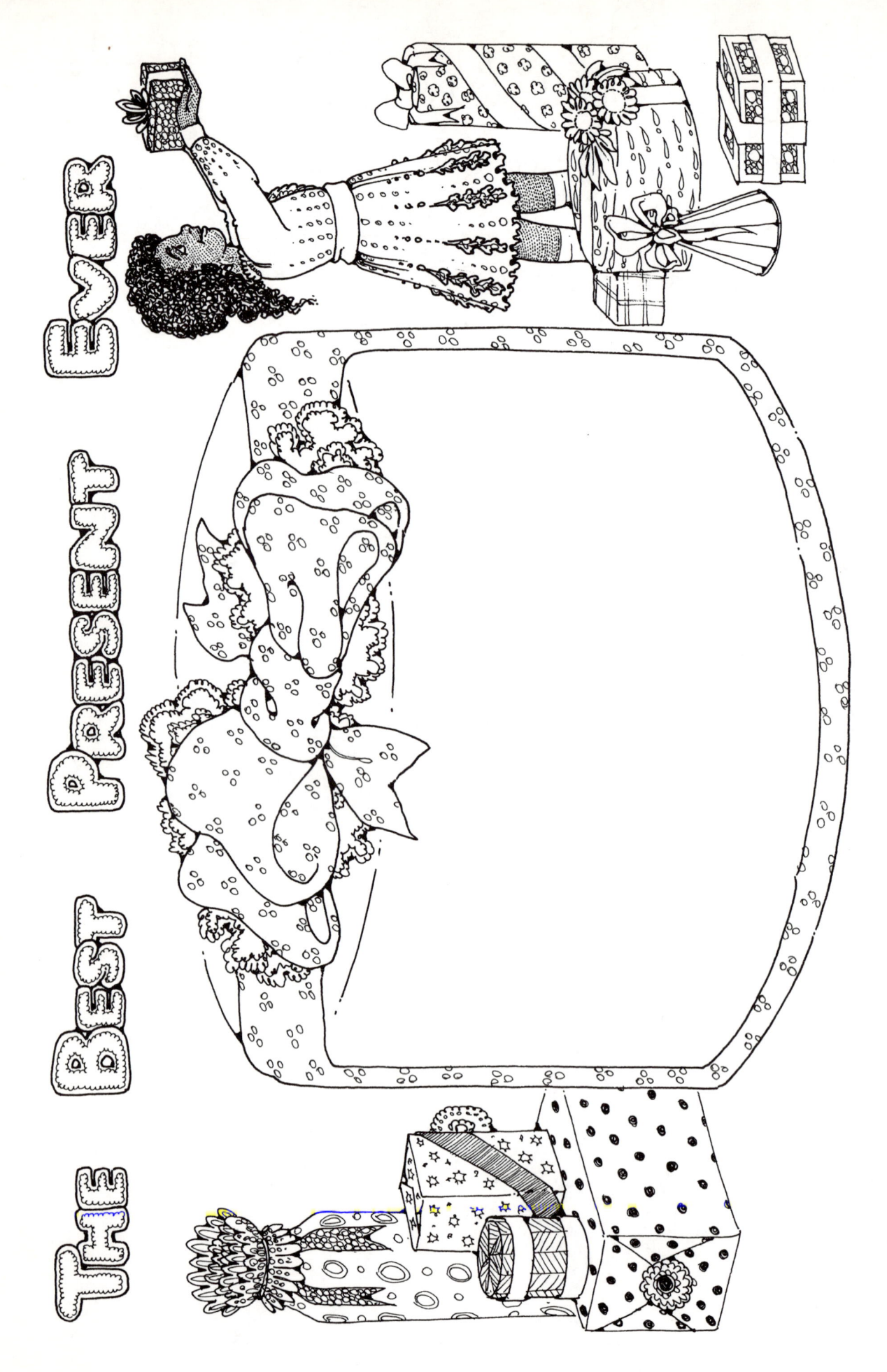

Draw or write about your best present ever.

What can I give that I don't have to buy?

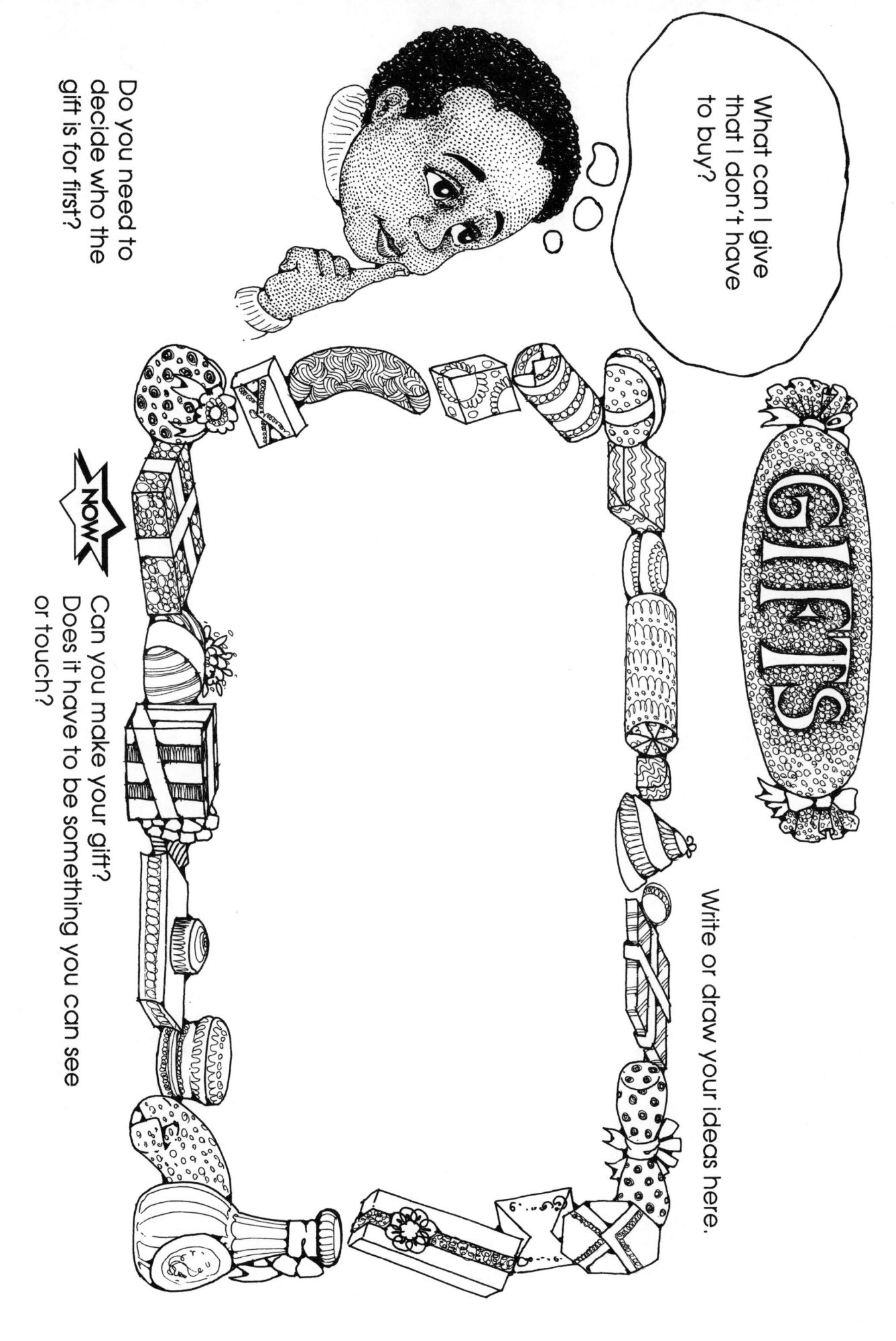

Do you need to decide who the gift is for first?

NOW

Can you make your gift? Does it have to be something you can see or touch?

GIFTS

Write or draw your ideas here.

SPECIAL PLACES

Draw or write about a place that is special to you. Why is it so special?

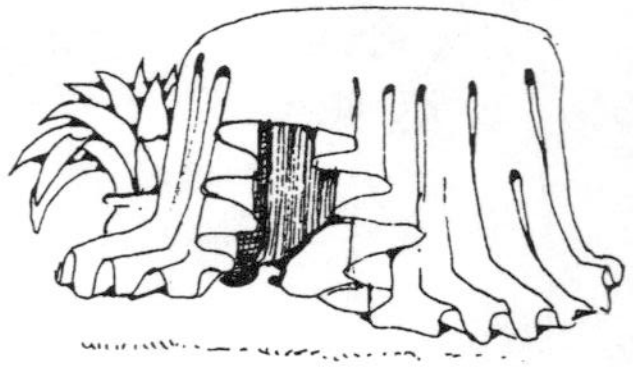

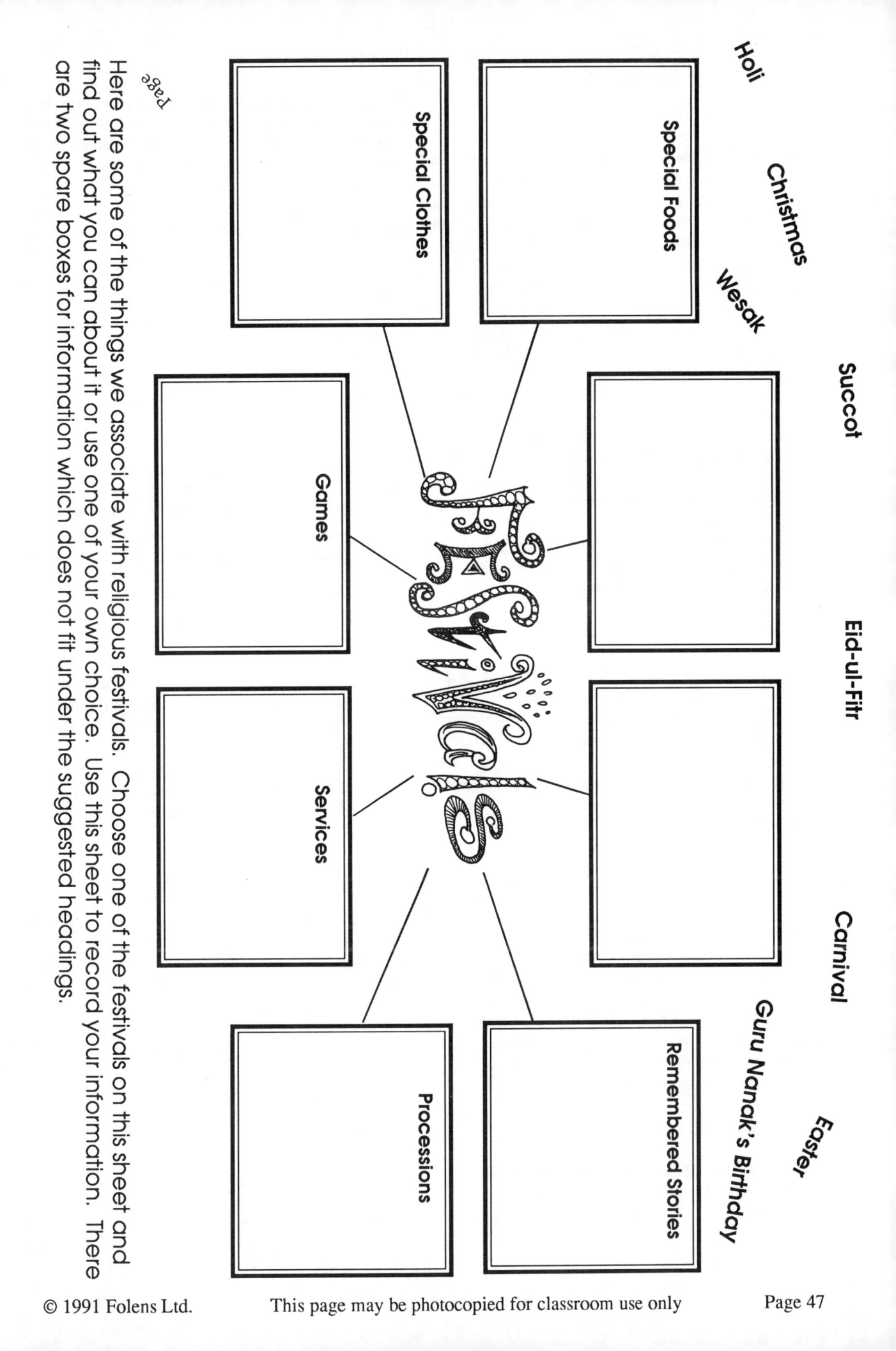

Festivals

Holi   Christmas   Wesak   Succot   Eid-ul-Fitr   Carnival   Guru Nanak's Birthday   Easter

- Special Foods
- Special Clothes
- Games
- Services
- Processions
- Remembered Stories

Here are some of the things we associate with religious festivals. Choose one of the festivals on this sheet and find out what you can about it or use one of your own choice. Use this sheet to record your information. There are two spare boxes for information which does not fit under the suggested headings.

© 1991 Folens Ltd.   This page may be photocopied for classroom use only   Page 47

SORROW

As we have already indicated, some celebrations are marked by a feeling of sorrow. It is important for children to realise that celebration and sorrow are not mutually exclusive, that to celebrate means above all else 'to affirm the worth of something' and not necessarily 'to be happy about'. In the children's own experience this may first become clear through the remembering of the anniversary of the death of a grandparent or perhaps by attending a funeral service. In the explicitly religious world it is seen in such Jewish celebrations as Yom Kippur and the annual remembrance of the Shoah (Holocaust), in the Christian celebration of Good Friday and the days of martyr saints, and in Sikh celebrations of the martyrdom of Guru Arjan and Guru Tegh Bahadur. It is also shown through the practice of fasting in which things of religious importance are celebrated through abstinence. But underpinning their ability to appreciate any such celebration is the children's own experience of sorrow in terms of both sadness and regret and their developing ability to identify with the sorrows and suffering of others, so it is there that an exploration of this area should begin.

Page 50 - What makes me sad?

This simple sheet offers even the youngest children the opportunity to consider what makes them sad. It is important to recognize that sadness is a universal human emotion and children can appreciate the sadness of others both by sharing their thoughts on the causes of their sadness and by recognizing that even adults (eg their parents) experience such feelings. To appreciate the universality of sadness is to begin to come to terms with it. Like happiness, sadness can be expressed in a variety of non-verbal ways. Children may explore this through such things as music, mime and bodily movement.

For some children, discussion of sadness will lead to a consideration of bereavement, an experience from which we cannot and should not seek to shield children totally. Seeing a sad parent, for example, and not being allowed to share in that sadness can result in a child feeling isolated and insecure. Children need to share in the sadness of bereavement if they are not to think of it as an emotion only for adults and thus something to be feared in later life.

A way in through story:

Amos J., *Sad* (Feelings series), Cherrytree Books
Gould D., *Grandpa's Slide Show*, Viking Kestrel
Krasilovsky P., *The Shy Little Girl*, World's Work

Page 51 - It makes me cry

This sheet extends the thinking of the previous one by focusing on the difference between physical and inner, emotional 'hurt'. 'Sticks and stones may break your bones but words can never hurt you' has to be one of the most untrue of all proverbs, and if children are to take responsibility for the consequences of their actions it is important for them to recognize that inner hurt can last longer than an outer bruise. This is true not only for them but also for those whom they can hurt by their words and actions.

A way in through story:

Amos J., *Hurt* (Feelings series), Cherrytree Books
Greenfield E., *Grandpa's Face*, Hutchinson
Keller H., *Goodbye Max*, Walker Books

Page 52 - I hurt someone

Here children are encouraged to reflect on themselves not as the victims of hurt and thus of sadness but as the possible causers of hurt to others. But, as with the previous sheet, it explores not just physical but also emotional hurt. Something I said (or forgot to say), did (or forgot to do) can cause hurt. Teachers familiar with the explicit world of religion will recognise here the basis for a mature understanding of the concept of confession. Before you can confess you must recognise that you have been the cause of 'hurt' to some other party and the 'sin' which you confess may be of commission or omission.

A second purpose of this sheet, however, is to prompt thinking about ways in which a hurt may be 'put right'. Saying 'sorry' is important, but there are many ways of doing it. Words (spoken or written), a gift, or a hand-shake may all convey that same message. To understand how human relationships are healed (how human 'hurts' are overcome) is a pre-requisite for later thinking about the healing of divine-human relationships and such concepts as grace, redemption, salvation, forgiveness, absolution etc. In both inter-human and human-divine relationships saying sorry (and being sorry) is the basis for forgiveness and for beginning again.

A way in through story:

Hughes S., *The Trouble with Jack*, Bodley Head
Kaye G., *King of the Knockdown Gingers*, Hodder and Stoughton.

Page 53 - Here is the news

This sheet seeks to transfer children's attention away from their own sadness and to encourage recognition of and empathy with that of others. Most children have some

© 1991 Folens Ltd.

awareness of major national and international events through the media. A significant number of these events involve the suffering of individuals or large numbers of people and children are often invited (eg through Blue Peter appeals) to respond in a practical way. Children should be helped to see that the media coverage of such events is a way of affirming the worth of the people involved, an idea (see above) essential to the concept of celebration, and they may also feel that attempts to relieve suffering are in themselves worthy of celebration. Important related issues are appreciation of the fact that the sharing of sad news is one step in the process of coming to terms with it and that empathy with the suffering of others promotes resolve that the suffering should not be allowed to recur - important themes in the Jews' annual remembrance of the Holocaust.

A possible way in:

Discussion of 'Newsround' (BBC TV)

Page 54 - Lasting memory

Central to this sheet is the idea of people who have had a lasting effect on the lives of others. Children are invited to think of somebody they will always remember. Try to help them to think of the reason for the lasting memory. It may be that they have been taught a skill or an attitude they will always retain. This is then extended to thought about those who will be remembered for their wider influence, particularly in the relief of suffering. A rich supply of examples can be found in the Faith in Action series published by R.M.E.P. though other modern examples (eg Bob Geldof, the Princess Royal) may come more readily to the children's minds and are equally appropriate. The work of such people is worthy of celebration and thus illustrates the fact that the ideas of sad memories and celebration are not mutually exclusive, a fact important to a number of religious celebrations.

A way in through story:

Selby J., *The Day Grandma Died*, Benjamin Books
Varley S., *Badger's Parting Gifts*, Picture Lion
Zolotow C., *My Grandson, Lew*, World's Work

Useful teacher and pupil resources:

Faith in Action series, R.M.E.P.
People Who Have Helped The World Series, Exley

Page 55 - A Time to Reflect

The sombre side of celebration appears in a variety of forms. One is in periods set aside for reflection in which the focus of attention is on repentance and new resolve and on the suffering of others. Many Christians use Lent in this way. It is not as complete a fast as Ramadan, though many Christians do practise various forms of abstinence throughout Lent. In addition to remembering Jesus' period of testing in the wilderness (Matthew 4: 1-11; Luke 4: 1-13), Christians often use this period to examine the quality of their own lives and to reflect on the suffering of others.

The Ten Days of Repentance at the beginning of the Jewish year (the period from Rosh Hashanah to Yom Kippur) serves a comparable function for practising Jews. Two themes merge in Jews' thinking at this period - creation and judgement. At this time Jews seek pardon for wrongs committed in the previous year and resolve to follow the requirements of the Torah (Law) more fully. The climax of this period, Yom Kippur, is a day of fasting symbolizing repentance.

For Muslims, Ramadan provides the opportunity both to give thanks for Muhammad's reception of the Qur'an and to engage in personal devotion which includes recognition of the needs of the poor and of those who suffer. In the hours of daylight - and children need to remember that Islam follows a lunar calendar; festivals rotate gradually around the solar year so Ramadan may fall in summer or winter - devout Muslims abstain from all food and drink, so the fast represents a major undertaking.

In addition to offering the opportunity to learn about these times of reflection, this final sheet invites children to engage in their own personal reflection. A quiet room is essential and a suitable atmosphere can be created by darkness pierced by a single lighted candle. If this is to be successful, it is important that some, at least, of the children's ideas are followed up. To arouse sympathy and concern and then to deny them an outlet is frustrating and unsatisfying for the children.

Relevant pupil resources are listed on page 40 ('Festivals'), page 31 ('New Year Celebrations') and page 15 ('Thanksgiving').

© 1991 Folens Ltd.

What Makes Me Sad?

I am sad when......

NOW

Ask your Mum and Dad what makes them sad.
What did they say?

Draw or use sticky paper to make this a sad face.

Cut out the face.

Turn it over and make it happy.

IT MAKES ME CRY

It hurts on the outside.

It hurts on the inside.

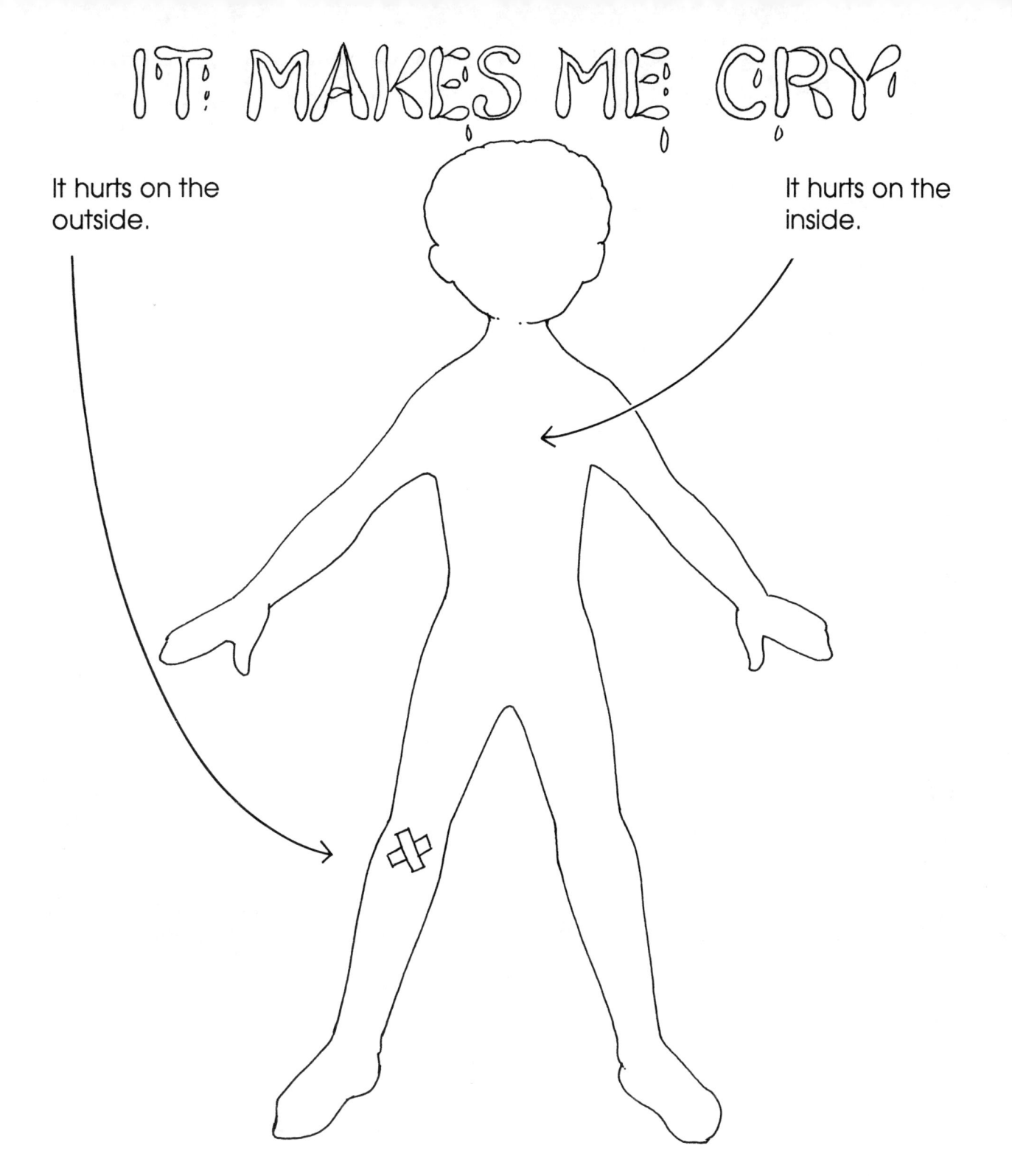

NOW Draw in the face and show where you might be hurt on the outside. Then write or tell about some of the things which hurt you on the inside.

I HURT SOMEONE

I forgot _____
_____
_____

I upset _____
_____
_____

I was unkind _____
_____
_____

I said _____
_____
_____

I'm sorry...

NOW Can you find a way of showing how sorry you are?

© 1991 Folens Ltd.   This page may be photocopied for classroom use only   Page 52

HERE IS THE NEWS

Much of what we see on television or read in the newspapers is sad news. Can you think of some examples? Can you think of any sad stories you have read recently?

Write about one or cut out an example from a newspaper or magazine and stick it here.

NOW

Can you tell a friend why this story or news item makes you sad? Does it help to share sad news?

With friends find a way to show your sadness in dance, mime or drama, painting, poetry or story.

LASTING MEMORY

Think of somebody you will always remember and say why you will remember them.

A PERSON I WILL REMEMBER

People may be remembered for many different reasons. Some are remembered for the way they have changed people's lives or a country's laws.

Try to think of some examples of people who have tried to do something about the suffering of other people. Choose one and say why what that person did was so important and has not been forgotten.

SOMEONE WHO HAS TRIED TO DO SOMETHING ABOUT SUFFERING

Name _____

Reasons for importance _____

_____

_____

_____

_____

© 1991 Folens Ltd.   This page may be photocopied for classroom use only

A time to reflect

In many religions you will find that there is a special time for people to think about the quality of their own lives, to express sorrow for the wrong they have done, to make resolutions for the future and to think about the sorrow and suffering of other people. For example:

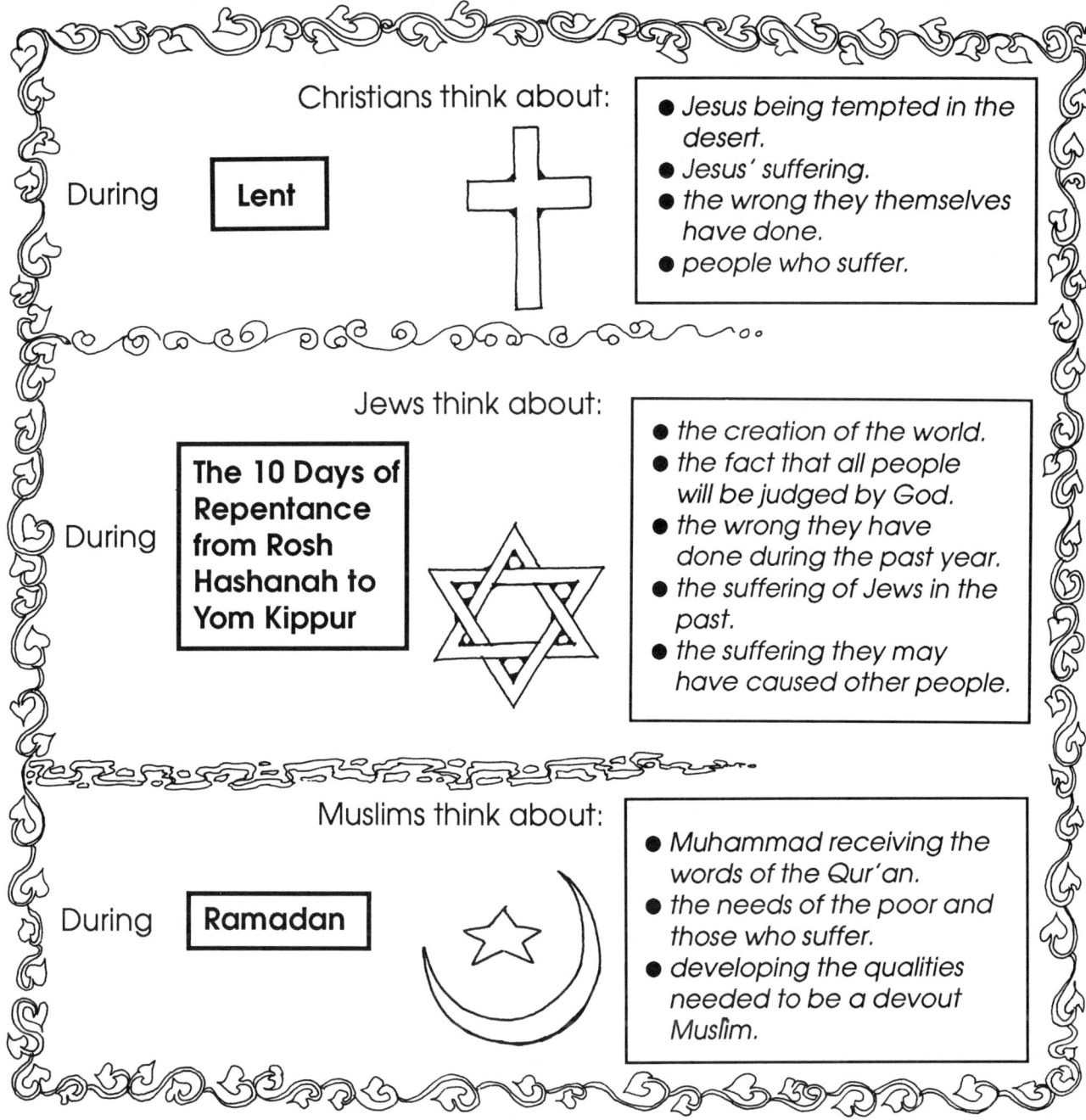

During **Lent**, Christians think about:
- *Jesus being tempted in the desert.*
- *Jesus' suffering.*
- *the wrong they themselves have done.*
- *people who suffer.*

During **The 10 Days of Repentance from Rosh Hashanah to Yom Kippur**, Jews think about:
- *the creation of the world.*
- *the fact that all people will be judged by God.*
- *the wrong they have done during the past year.*
- *the suffering of Jews in the past.*
- *the suffering they may have caused other people.*

During **Ramadan**, Muslims think about:
- *Muhammad receiving the words of the Qur'an.*
- *the needs of the poor and those who suffer.*
- *developing the qualities needed to be a devout Muslim.*

Find out what you can about these periods of reflection and report to the rest of the class.

NOW Time to think

- Are you prepared to give up anything to remind you of the suffering of others?
- Have you hurt anyone today? What can you do about it?
- What can you do to help those who are suffering? Is there anything you can do to prevent the suffering?

© 1991 Folens Ltd. This page may be photocopied for classroom use only

ADDITIONAL TEACHER RESOURCES

Bailey J., *Primary R.E. Materials: Islam* - A series of eight information wallets published jointly by the Centre for the Study of Islam and Christian-Muslim Relations and the Regional R.E. Centre (Midlands)

Barratt M. et al, *Attainment in R.E.: A Handbook for Teachers,* The Regional R.E. Centre (Midlands), Westhill College

Bechely P., (ed.), *Something to Think About,* BBC

Bennett O., *Festivals: Exploring Religion* series (includes Chanukah, Easter, Christmas and Divali), Bell and Hyman

Broadbent L., *Exploring a Theme: Spring Festivals* (includes Chinese New Year, Holi, Purim, Passover and Easter) - and other volumes in the series, C.E.M.

Cato P. and Washford Murphy R., *Brain Waves: First Topics,* Folens

Cato P. and Washford Murphy R., *Brain Waves: Exploring Themes,* Folens

Doyle M et al, *Hinduism: Religious and Multi-Cultural Education Resource Material,* Selly Oak Colleges and the Regional R.E. Centre (Midlands), Westhill College

Gavin J., *The Magic Orange Tree,* Magnet

Gilbert J., *Festivals,* O.U.P., Music Department

Gregory R., *Thirty Stories for Infant R.E.,* Bedfordshire Education Service

Gregory R., *Fifteen Stories for Junior R.E.,* Bedfordshire Education Service

Grimmitt M. et al., *A Gift to the Child,* Simon and Schuster

Jaffrey M., *Seasons of Splendour: Tales, Myths and Legends of India,* Puffin

Lynch M., Teachers' notes to accompany Ginn *Celebrations* series

Mayled J., *Jewish Festivals - Teacher's Book,* R.M.E.P.

Mayled J., *Christian Festivals - Teacher's Book,* R.M.E.P.

Rankin J. Brown A. and Hayward M., *Religious Education Topics for the Primary School,* Longman

Stevens M. and Brown R., *Religious Education Through Stories,* Leicestershire Education Committee

Taylor D., *Exploring Red Letter Days,* Lutterworth

Vause D., *The Infant Assembly Book,* Macdonald

My Belief series, Franklin Watts.